THE KINGFISHER
Children's
ATLAS

KINGFISHER

BOSTON

KINGFISHER

a Houghton Mifflin Company imprint
222 Berkeley Street
Boston, Massachusetts 02116
www.houghtonmifflinbooks.com

Written by
Belinda Weber

Senior editor: Catherine Brereton
Coordinating editor: Caitlin Doyle
Art director: Mike Davis
Designer: Anthony Cutting
Assistant designer: Chloe Aylward
Cartographic consultant: Jan Clark
Picture researcher: Rachael Swann
DTP coordinator: Jonathan Pledge
DTP operator: Primrose Burton
Senior production controller: Lindsey Scott
Artwork archivists: Wendy Allison, Jenny Lord
Proofreader: Sheila Clewley
Indexer: Jan Clark
Additional research: Mike Davis
Cover designed by: Mike Davis

Cartography by: Anderson Geographics Limited,
Warfield, Berkshire, U.K.

First published in 2004
1 3 5 7 9 10 8 6 4 2
1TR/0504/TIMS/CLSN(CLSN)/128MA/F

LIBRARY OF CONGRESS CATALOGING-IN-PUBLICATION DATA
has been applied for.

ISBN 0-7534-5774-1

Printed in China

CONTENTS

Earth   4–5
Using maps   6–7
Countries of the world   8–9

NORTH AMERICA 10–11
Canada   12–13
Western U.S.   14–15
Eastern U.S.   16–17
Central America   18–19
The Caribbean   20–21

SOUTH AMERICA 22–23
Northern South America   24–25
Southern South America   26–27

EUROPE   28–29
Northwestern Europe   30–31
The British Isles   32–33
Germany and the
  Low Countries   34–35
France   36–37
Spain and Portugal   38–39
The Alpine States
  and Italy   40–41
Eastern and
  Central Europe   42–43
Southeastern Europe   44–45

ASIA   52–53
The Russian Federation   54–55
West Asia   56–57
Central Asia   58–59
South Asia   60–61
Southeast Asia   62–63
East Asia   64–65
Japan and the Koreas   66–67

AUSTRALASIA
& OCEANIA   68–69
Australia   70–71
New Zealand   72

The Poles   73

Facts and figures   74–75
Index   76–79
Acknowledgments   80

AFRICA   46–47
Northern Africa   48–49
Central and Southern Africa   50–51

EARTH

Earth is a planet that rotates around the Sun. It is covered with huge landmasses, called continents, and vast oceans and seas. There are seven continents: North America, South America, Europe, Africa, Asia, Australasia and Oceania, and Antarctica. Most of them have a variety of different types of landscapes. There are high, mountainous regions and low-lying plains. Where there is little or no rain, deserts are found. Flowing rivers can bring an abundance of animal and plant life to an area, and they also cut paths through the landscape. In areas with high rainfall rain forests can grow, providing lush green oases.

Humans also influence the landscape. We farm the land and build villages, towns, and huge cities with skyscrapers for people to live and work in.

Shaping the world

Humans also shape the landscape by dividing up the land into countries. Some countries are whole islands, but most are parts of the larger landmasses. Often mountains or rivers mark the boundaries between countries, but sometimes there is nothing physical to mark the border where one country ends and another begins. Humans live on almost every area of land on the planet. Currently there are around 6.34 billion people living in the world.

Mountain ranges
Mountains reach high up toward the sky. The higher up you go, the colder the temperature. Very few animals can live at the top.

Sandy deserts
In places with little or no rain deserts, such as the Sahara, form. This sandy wilderness covers much of northern Africa.

Winding rivers
Rivers and streams wind their way through the landscape on their way to the sea. They can carve paths through solid rock.

Green and wet
Tropical rain forests grow in hot, rainy areas, carpeting the land with a rich variety of plant life. Animals thrive in these forests.

Maps and mapping

We use maps and globes to show and find out about the countries of the world. A globe is a ball with all the continents and oceans drawn on it. A map is a flat plan of the world. Imagine that you had an orange with all the countries and seas drawn on it. If you peeled it and laid the peel out flat, you would get an uneven shape. Mapmakers make a whole picture by stretching the shape of some of the countries and seas.

Mapmakers also draw imaginary lines across Earth's surface. Lines around Earth are called lines of latitude. Lines going from the top to the bottom are called lines of longitude. These form a grid over Earth's surface that help us pinpoint exactly where in the world a place is.

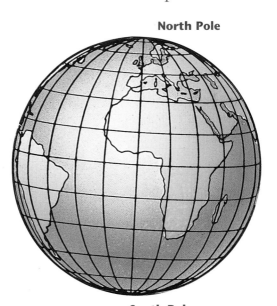

North Pole

South Pole

Pole to pole
Lines going from the top to the bottom are called lines of longitude. All the lines of longitude meet at the North and South poles, which are the most northerly and southerly points on Earth.

Greenwich Meridian
The line of longitude in the middle of Earth is called the Greenwich Meridian.

Equator
Lines around Earth are called lines of latitude. The equator is a line of latitude around the middle of Earth.

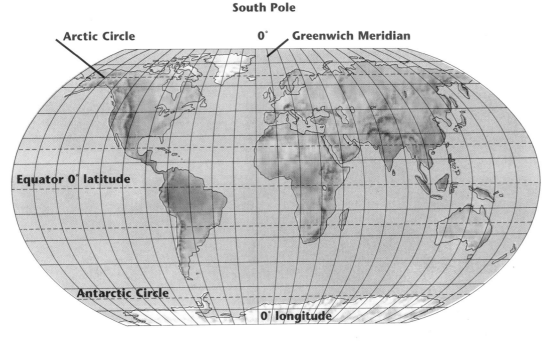

Arctic Circle   0°   Greenwich Meridian

Equator 0° latitude

Antarctic Circle

0° longitude

Concrete jungles
Humans build huge cities to house millions of people. These urban buildings change the look of what was once a natural landscape.

Using maps

An atlas is a book of maps. Maps are pictures that tell us about different places. They provide all types of useful information about countries. Maps use different colors, symbols, and lines to show mountains and valleys, oceans and seas, and rivers and lakes. On most of the maps in this atlas, like the example below, colors are also used to show the height of the land above sea level. Some maps use colors to show different types of information such as where there are fertile places and deserts.

Red lines on the maps show where one country starts and another one ends. These lines are called borders. Squares represent capital cities. A capital is the main city in a country, where the government and other important organizations are based. A few countries have more than one capital. All other towns and cities on the maps are marked with red dots. The maps in this atlas also have picture symbols that show you where to find animals, industry, landmarks, and a variety of places of interest.

The maps in this atlas use a set of symbols and words to mark different types of features. This key shows you what they all mean.

Settlements

■ CARACAS Capital city
■ Denver State capital city
● Manaus Major city or town
• Maturín Other city or town

Political and cultural regions

BRAZIL Country

Aruba Dependent territory
(to Netherlands)

ARIZONA State, province, or national region

Boundaries

International border

Disputed border

State, province, or national regional boundary

Drainage features

River

Seasonal river

Canal

Waterfall

Lake

Seasonal lake

Topographic features

Δ *Cotopaxi 19,342 ft.* Height of mountain

Isla de Marájo Island/island group

Amazon Basin Physical feature/ landscape region

Seas and oceans

PACIFIC OCEAN Name of ocean

Caribbean Sea Name of sea

Sea

Ice features

Limit of summer pack ice

Limit of winter pack ice

Land height

4,000m 13,124 ft.

2,000m 6,562 ft.

1,000m 3,281 ft.

500m 1,640 ft.

200m 656 ft.

Sea level

Extra information

Next to the maps you will find symbols telling you more about the area covered in the map to help you understand where it fits in the world.

Equator

Flags

Every country in the world has its own national flag. You will find these flags throughout the atlas. They symbolize the country's independence and identity.

Globe

The globe on each page shows where the countries on the map are located in the world (marked in orange). Some of the map pages have an extra map in a small box called an inset. The position of these insets is shown by an orange box on the globe.

Scale bar

All the maps in this atlas have a scale bar. This will tell you how distances on the page relate to real distances on the ground. For example, the scale bar shown below tells you that one inch on the map represents 250 miles on the ground.

Grid

Around the edges of each page you will find a grid with letters and numbers. The index at the end of the book will give you a page number and grid reference. By using the grid reference, you will be able to find the particular town or city you are looking for.

Picture symbols

On the maps you will also find picture symbols that show interesting features in each country. Here are a few examples. Look out for more throughout the atlas.

Dairy cattle
An example of a farm animal

Fishing
An example of a type of industry

Toucan
An example of a type of wildlife

Catedral Basílica
An example of a famous building or landmark

Bananas
An example of a food crop

Countries of the world

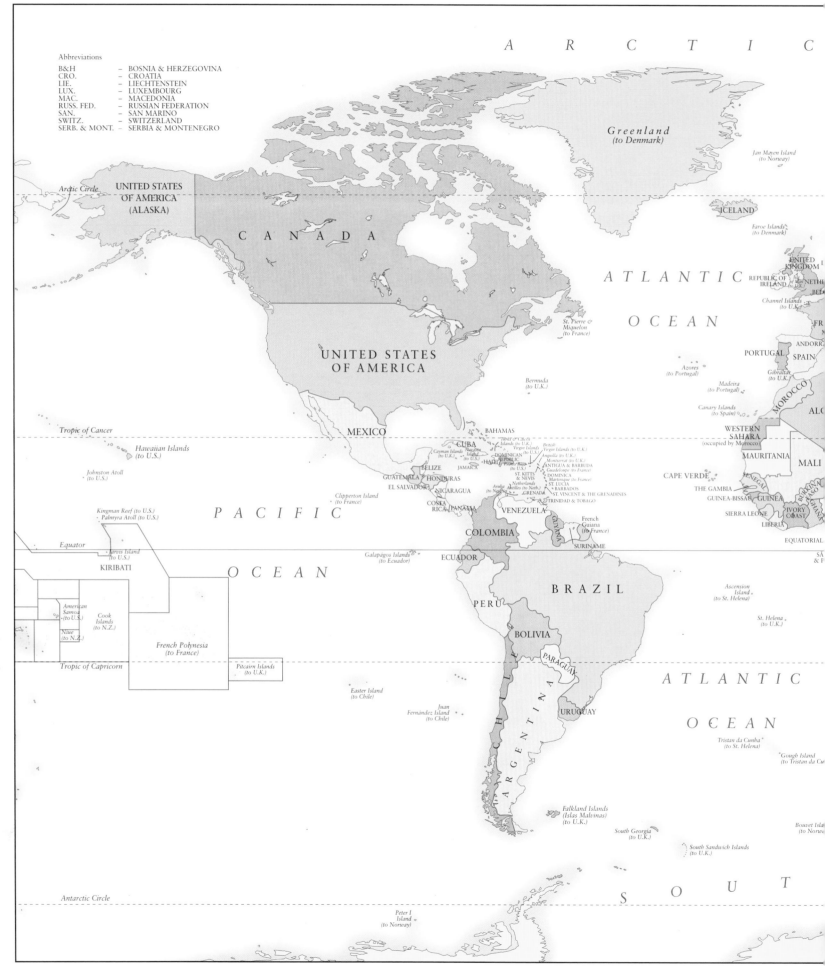

Abbreviations

Abbreviations
B&H   – BOSNIA & HERZEGOVINA
CRO.   – CROATIA
LIE.   – LIECHTENSTEIN
LUX.   – LUXEMBOURG
MAC.   – MACEDONIA
RUSS. FED.   – RUSSIAN FEDERATION
SAN.   – SAN MARINO
SWITZ.   – SWITZERLAND
SERB. & MONT. – SERBIA & MONTENEGRO

A R C T I C

Greenland
(to Denmark)

Jan Mayen Island
(to Norway)

Arctic Circle

UNITED STATES
OF AMERICA
(ALASKA)

ICELAND

C A N A D A

Faroe Islands
(to Denmark)

A T L A N T I C

UNITED
KINGDOM

REPUBLIC OF
IRELAND

NETH

St. Pierre &
Miquelon
(to France)

O C E A N

Channel Islands
(to U.K.)

FR

UNITED STATES
OF AMERICA

ANDORR

PORTUGAL   SPAIN

Azores
(to Portugal)

Gibraltar
(to U.K.)

Madeira
(to Portugal)

Tropic of Cancer

MEXICO

BAHAMAS

Canary Islands
(to Spain)

MOROCCO

WESTERN
SAHARA
(occupied by Morocco)

AL

CUBA

Hawaiian Islands
(to U.S.)

Turks & Caicos
Islands (to U.K.)
Cayman Islands
(to U.K.)

JAMAICA

Virgin Islands
(to U.S.)
HAITI

British
Virgin Islands (to U.K.)
Anguilla (to U.K.)
ANTIGUA & BARBUDA

MAURITANIA

MALI

Johnston Atoll
(to U.S.)

GUATEMALA

DOMINICAN
REPUBLIC
(to U.S.)

HONDURAS

Montserrat (to U.K.)
Guadeloupe (to France)
DOMINICA
Martinique (to France)
ST. LUCIA

ST. KITTS
& NEVIS

CAPE VERDE

Kingman Reef (to U.S.)
Palmyra Atoll (to U.S.)

EL SALVADOR

Clipperton Island
(to France)

NICARAGUA

COSTA
RICA   PANAMA

Netherlands
Antilles (to Neth.)
Aruba
(to Neth.)

BARBADOS
ST. VINCENT & THE GRENADINES
GRENADA

THE GAMBIA

GUINEA-BISSAU   GUINEA

SENEGAL
BURKINA
FASO

P A C I F I C

VENEZUELA

TRINIDAD & TOBAGO

GUYANA

French
Guiana
(to France)

SIERRA LEONE

IVORY
COAST

GHAN

LIBERIA

EQUATORIAL

Equator

Jarvis Island
(to U.S.)

O C E A N

Galápagos Islands
(to Ecuador)

COLOMBIA

ECUADOR

SURINAME

SÃ
F

KIRIBATI

Ascension
Island
(to St. Helena)

American
Samoa
(to U.S.)

Cook
Islands
(to N.Z.)

PERU

B R A Z I L

Niue
(to N.Z.)

French Polynesia
(to France)

BOLIVIA

St. Helena
(to U.K.)

Tropic of Capricorn

Pitcairn Islands
(to U.K.)

PARAGUAY

A T L A N T I C

Easter Island
(to Chile)

Juan
Fernández Island
(to Chile)

URUGUAY

O C E A N

Tristan da Cunha
(to St. Helena)

CHILE

ARGENTINA

Gough Island
(to Tristan da Cu

Falkland Islands
(Islas Malvinas)
(to U.K.)

Bouvet Isla
(to Norw

South Georgia
(to U.K.)

South Sandwich Islands
(to U.K.)

S O U T

Antarctic Circle

Peter I
Island
(to Norway)

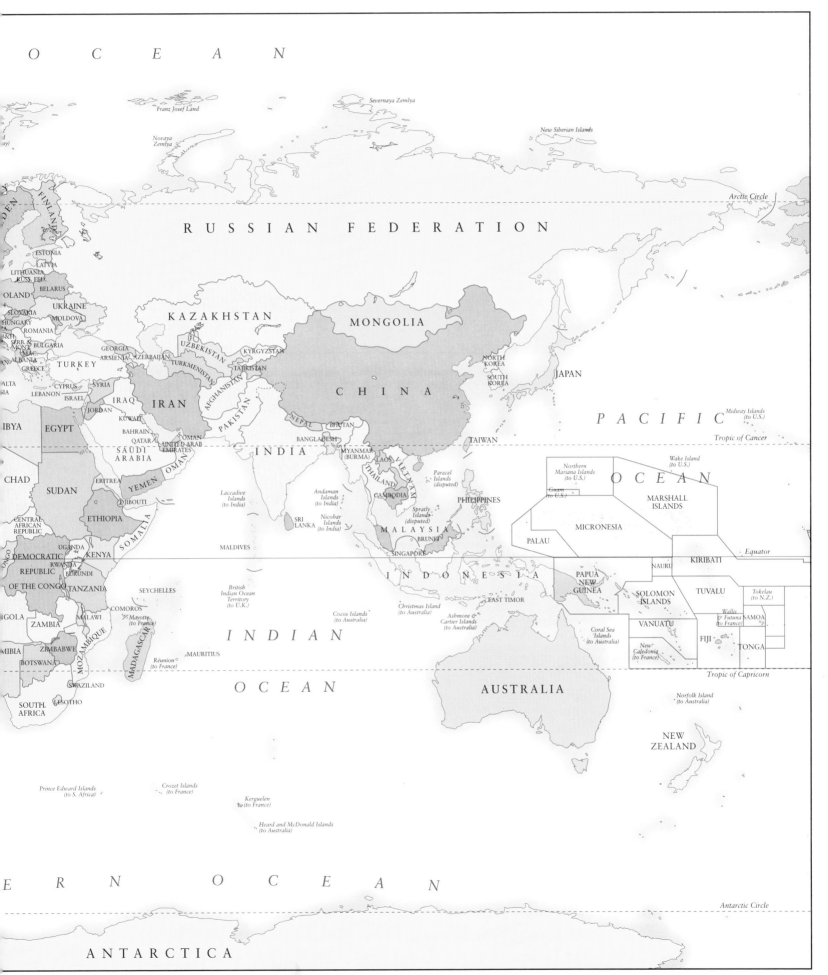

O C E A N

Franz Josef Land

Novaya Zemlya

Severnaya Zemlya

New Siberian Islands

DEN

FINLAND

ESTONIA
LATVIA
LITHUANIA
RUSS. FED.
BELARUS

POLAND

SLOVAKIA
HUNGARY
ROMANIA
SERB. &
MONT.
MAC.
BULGARIA
ALBANIA
GREECE

MALTA

CYPRUS
LEBANON
ISRAEL
JORDAN

TURKEY

GEORGIA
ARMENIA AZERBAIJAN

SYRIA

IRAQ

KUWAIT

LIBYA

EGYPT

BAHRAIN
QATAR
UNITED ARAB
EMIRATES
SAUDI
ARABIA

CHAD

SUDAN

ERITREA

YEMEN
DJIBOUTI

CENTRAL
AFRICAN
REPUBLIC

ETHIOPIA

CONGO
DEMOCRATIC
REPUBLIC
OF THE CONGO

UGANDA
RWANDA
BURUNDI

KENYA

TANZANIA

SOMALIA

ANGOLA

ZAMBIA

MALAWI

COMOROS

SEYCHELLES

NAMIBIA

ZIMBABWE

BOTSWANA

MOZAMBIQUE

SWAZILAND

SOUTH
AFRICA

LESOTHO

MADAGASCAR

*Mayotte
(to France)*

*Réunion
(to France)*

MAURITIUS

RUSSIAN FEDERATION

Arctic Circle

KAZAKHSTAN

UZBEKISTAN

KYRGYZSTAN

TURKMENISTAN

TAJIKISTAN

IRAN

AFGHANISTAN

PAKISTAN

MONGOLIA

CHINA

NORTH
KOREA

SOUTH
KOREA

JAPAN

NEPAL

BHUTAN

INDIA

BANGLADESH

MYANMAR
(BURMA)

TAIWAN

Tropic of Cancer

OMAN

*Laccadive
Islands
(to India)*

*Andaman
Islands
(to India)*

LAOS

THAILAND

VIETNAM

*Paracel
Islands
(disputed)*

CAMBODIA

PHILIPPINES

PACIFIC

*Midway Islands
(to U.S.)*

*Wake Island
(to U.S.)*

O C E A N

*Northern
Mariana Islands
(to U.S.)*

*Guam
(to U.S.)*

MARSHALL
ISLANDS

SRI
LANKA

*Nicobar
Islands
(to India)*

*Spratly
Islands
(disputed)*

MALAYSIA

BRUNEI

MICRONESIA

PALAU

MALDIVES

SINGAPORE

I N D O N E S I A

Equator

NAURU

KIRIBATI

PAPUA
NEW
GUINEA

SOLOMON
ISLANDS

TUVALU

*Tokelau
(to N.Z.)*

*British
Indian Ocean
Territory
(to U.K.)*

*Christmas Island
(to Australia)*

EAST TIMOR

*Ashmore &
Cartier Islands
(to Australia)*

VANUATU

*Wallis &
Futuna
(to France)*

SAMOA

*Cocos Islands
(to Australia)*

*Coral Sea
Islands
(to Australia)*

*New
Caledonia
(to France)*

FIJI

TONGA

I N D I A N

O C E A N

AUSTRALIA

*Norfolk Island
(to Australia)*

Tropic of Capricorn

NEW
ZEALAND

*Prince Edward Islands
(to S. Africa)*

*Crozet Islands
(to France)*

*Kerguelen
(to France)*

*Heard and McDonald Islands
(to Australia)*

ERN   O C E A N

Antarctic Circle

A N T A R C T I C A

9

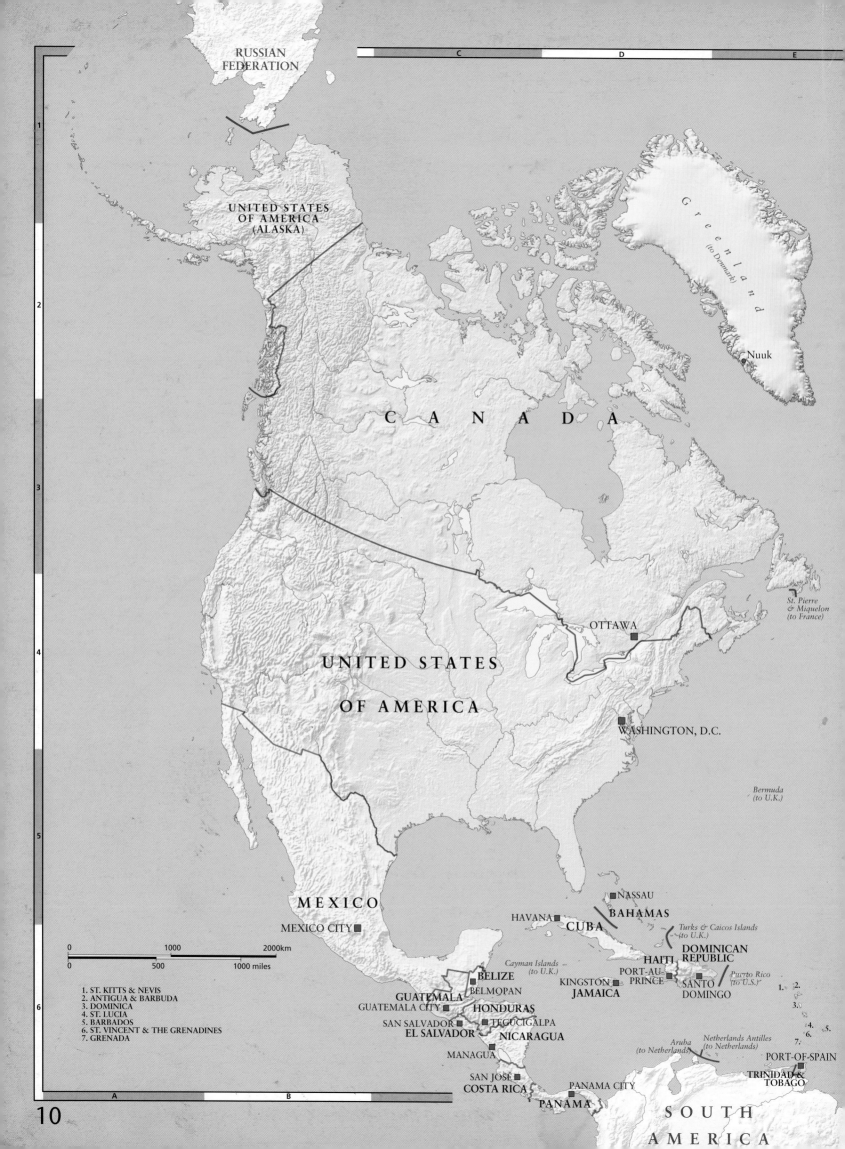

RUSSIAN
FEDERATION

UNITED STATES
OF AMERICA
(ALASKA)

Greenland
(to Denmark)

Nuuk

C A N A D A

St. Pierre
& Miquelon
(to France)

OTTAWA

UNITED STATES

OF AMERICA

WASHINGTON, D.C.

Bermuda
(to U.K.)

M E X I C O

MEXICO CITY

NASSAU

HAVANA   BAHAMAS

CUBA   *Turks & Caicos Islands*
          (to U.K.)

Cayman Islands   DOMINICAN
(to U.K.)   REPUBLIC

BELIZE   HAITI
BELMOPAN   PORT-AU-   *Puerto Rico*
KINGSTON   PRINCE   *(to U.S.)*
GUATEMALA   JAMAICA   SANTO
GUATEMALA CITY   DOMINGO   1.   2.

HONDURAS   3.
SAN SALVADOR   TEGUCIGALPA
EL SALVADOR   4.   5.
           NICARAGUA   6.
                                    7.
MANAGUA   *Aruba*   *Netherlands Antilles*
           (to Netherlands) *(to Netherlands)*
                                    PORT-OF-SPAIN

SAN JOSE   TRINIDAD &
COSTA RICA PANAMA CITY   TOBAGO

PANAMA   S O U T H

                        A M E R I C A

0   1000   2000km
0   500   1000 miles

1. ST. KITTS & NEVIS
2. ANTIGUA & BARBUDA
3. DOMINICA
4. ST. LUCIA
5. BARBADOS
6. ST. VINCENT & THE GRENADINES
7. GRENADA

10

Rich farmland
The Mississippi river carries sediment (tiny specks of mud) in its waters, which it leaves as fertile soil along its way. Many crops are grown on the plains beside the river.

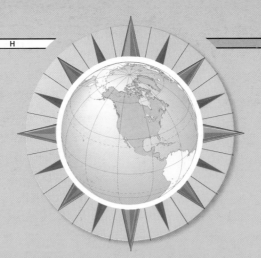

NORTH AMERICA

The continent of North America is the third-largest continent. It stretches from the frozen Arctic in the north to the tropics in the south. In the winter the far north is bitterly cold as icy winds blow off the Arctic. Most parts of the continent have warm or hot summers. The Rocky Mountains stretch along the west of the continent, reaching from northern Canada to Mexico. On the east of the continent lie the Appalachians, and in between these two mountain ranges are large, flat plains, across which the mighty Mississippi and Missouri rivers flow.

North America consists of three large countries—Canada, the United States of America, and Mexico— as well as the island of Greenland and the smaller countries of Central America and the Caribbean.

Crystal clear
Canada has more lakes and inland water than anywhere else in the world. Many national parks have been set up to protect the lakes and the areas surrounding them.

Thumbs-up!
People from many different cultures make up the United States of America. Settlers from Europe, Africa, and Asia, as well as the Native Americans, are all part of a multicultural society.

Canada

Canada is an enormous country—the second largest in the world after the Russian Federation. But most of Canada's 30 million people live in the south in cities along the border with the United States. Very few people live in the Northwest Territories or in the islands off the north coast since the lands here are inside the Arctic Circle, and temperatures can drop to a bitterly cold -40°F (-40°C). The Rocky Mountains in the west are covered with trees and are home to wildlife such as the bald eagle. In the far north there are polar bears. In the central areas there are vast plains, where large quantities of wheat are grown.

Half of Canada's population live along the St. Lawrence Seaway, close the Great Lakes. Canada has two official languages—French and English. Most of the French-speaking Canadians live in the province of Québec.

Long journey
Monarch butterflies from Canada gather in their thousands every fall and fly south. They spend the winter in Florida, southern California, and northern Mexico. Some travel more than 2,217 mi. (3,430km).

FACTS AND FIGURES

Largest cities
Toronto 4,683,000
Montreal 3,426,000

Longest river
Mackenzie 1,074 mi. (1,733km)

Largest lake
Lake Superior 32,117 sq. mi. (82,350km²). This is the largest lake in North America and the second largest in the world

Highest mountain
Mount Logan 19,850 ft. (5,959m)

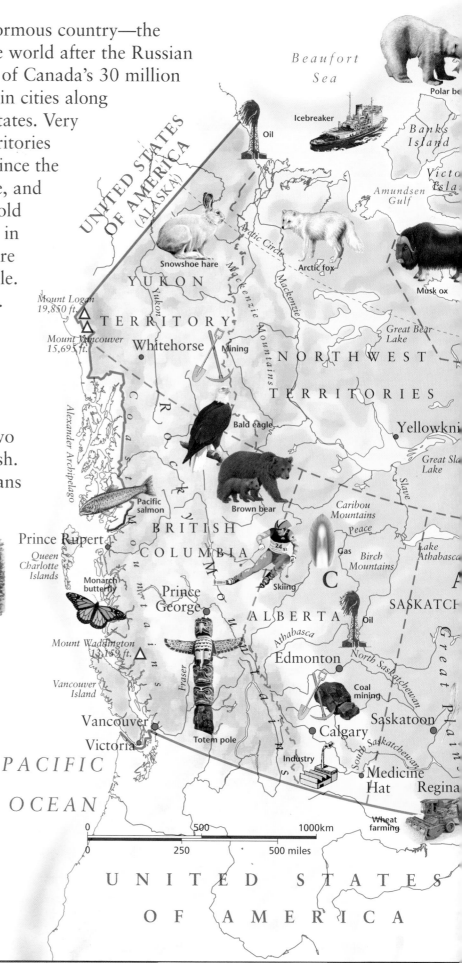

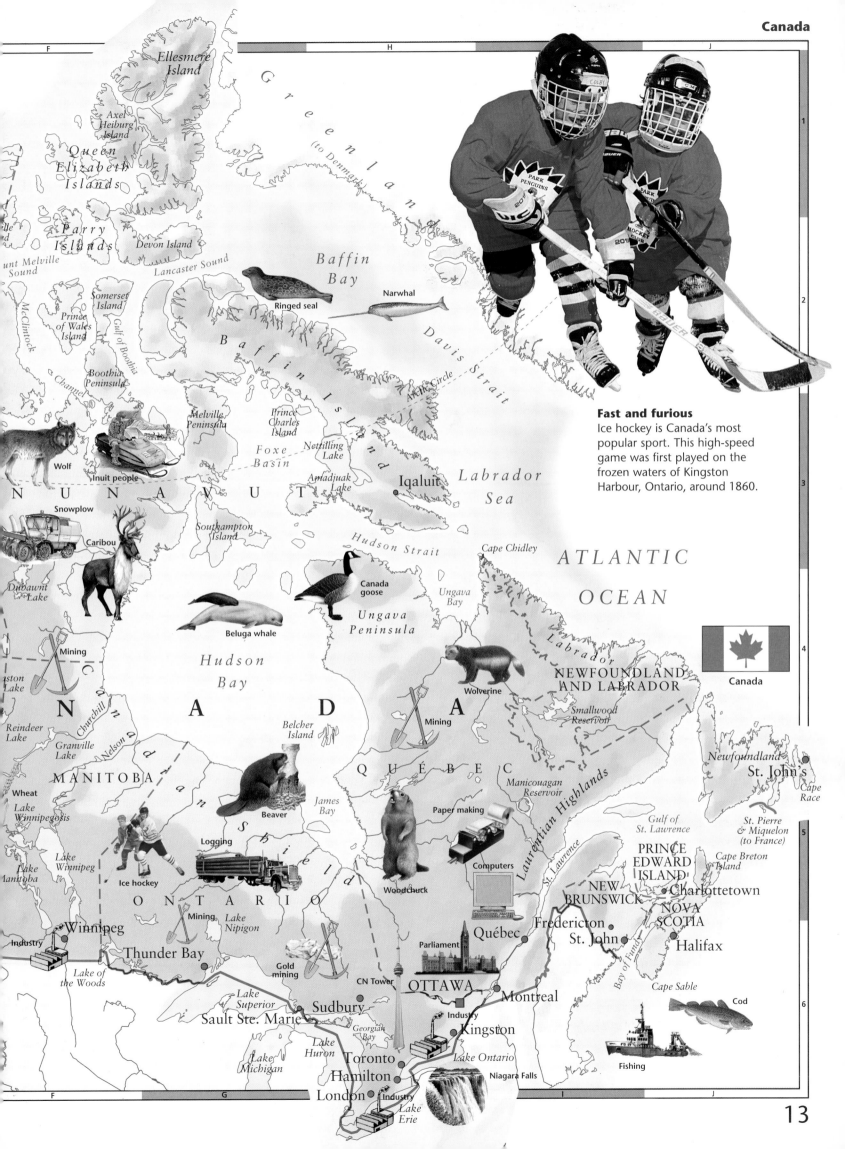

Ellesmere Island

Axel Heiburg Island

Queen Elizabeth Islands

Parry Islands

Devon Island

Somerset Island

Prince of Wales Island

Boothia Peninsula

McClintock Channel

Gulf of Boothia

Lancaster Sound

G r e e n l a n d (to Denmark)

Baffin Bay

Ringed seal

Narwhal

Davis Strait

Fast and furious

Ice hockey is Canada's most popular sport. This high-speed game was first played on the frozen waters of Kingston Harbour, Ontario, around 1860.

Melville Peninsula

Prince Charles Island

Foxe Basin

Nettilling Lake

Amadjuak Lake

Arctic Circle

Iqaluit

Labrador Sea

Wolf

Inuit people

N U N A V U T

Snowplow

Caribou

Dubawnt Lake

Hudson Strait

Cape Chidley

Ungava Bay

ATLANTIC OCEAN

Canada goose

Beluga whale

Ungava Peninsula

Mining

Hudson Bay

C

A

N

Churchill

Wolverine

Mining

Labrador

NEWFOUNDLAND AND LABRADOR

Canada

Smallwood Reservoir

Reindeer Lake

Granville Lake

Nelson

N

A

D

A

Belcher Island

Manicouagan Reservoir

Laurentian Highlands

Newfoundland

St. John's

Cape Race

MANITOBA

Wheat

Lake Winnipegosis

Lake Winnipeg

Lake Manitoba

Beaver

James Bay

Paper making

QUÉBEC

Gulf of St. Lawrence

St. Pierre & Miquelon (to France)

Cape Breton Island

Ice hockey

Logging

Woodchuck

Computers

O

N

T

A

R

I

O

Mining

Lake Nipigon

St. Lawrence

PRINCE EDWARD ISLAND

NEW BRUNSWICK

Charlottetown

NOVA SCOTIA

Winnipeg

Industry

Thunder Bay

Lake of the Woods

Gold mining

CN Tower

OTTAWA

Parliament

Québec

Fredericton

St. John

Halifax

Montreal

Bay of Fundy

Cape Sable

Cod

Sault Ste. Marie

Lake Superior

Sudbury

Georgian Bay

Industry

Kingston

Lake Huron

Toronto

Lake Michigan

Hamilton

Niagara Falls

Lake Ontario

Fishing

London

Industry

Lake Erie

13

Western U.S.

The United States of America occupies the central part of the continent of North America. This powerful country is divided up into 50 states. The land and climate across such a huge country vary greatly, from icy Arctic wilderness in Alaska to burning hot deserts in Arizona, swamps in the Everglades, and rolling grasslands in the prairies of the Midwest.

The western U.S. includes landmarks such as the Grand Canyon, a deep gorge carved out by the Colorado river. In California the climate is perfect for growing oranges. It is also the home of Silicon Valley, where microchips and electronic equipment are produced.

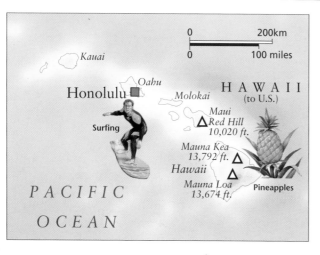

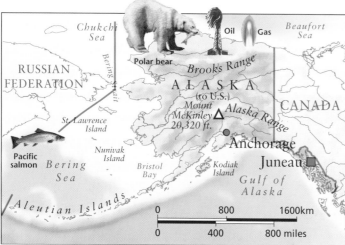

FACTS AND FIGURES

Largest cities
Los Angeles 3,798,981
Dallas 1,211,467

Largest state
Alaska

Longest river
Mississippi-Missouri 3,732 mi. (6,020km)

Highest mountain
Mount McKinley 20,320 ft. (6,194m)

Lowest point
Death Valley 282 ft. (86m) below sea level

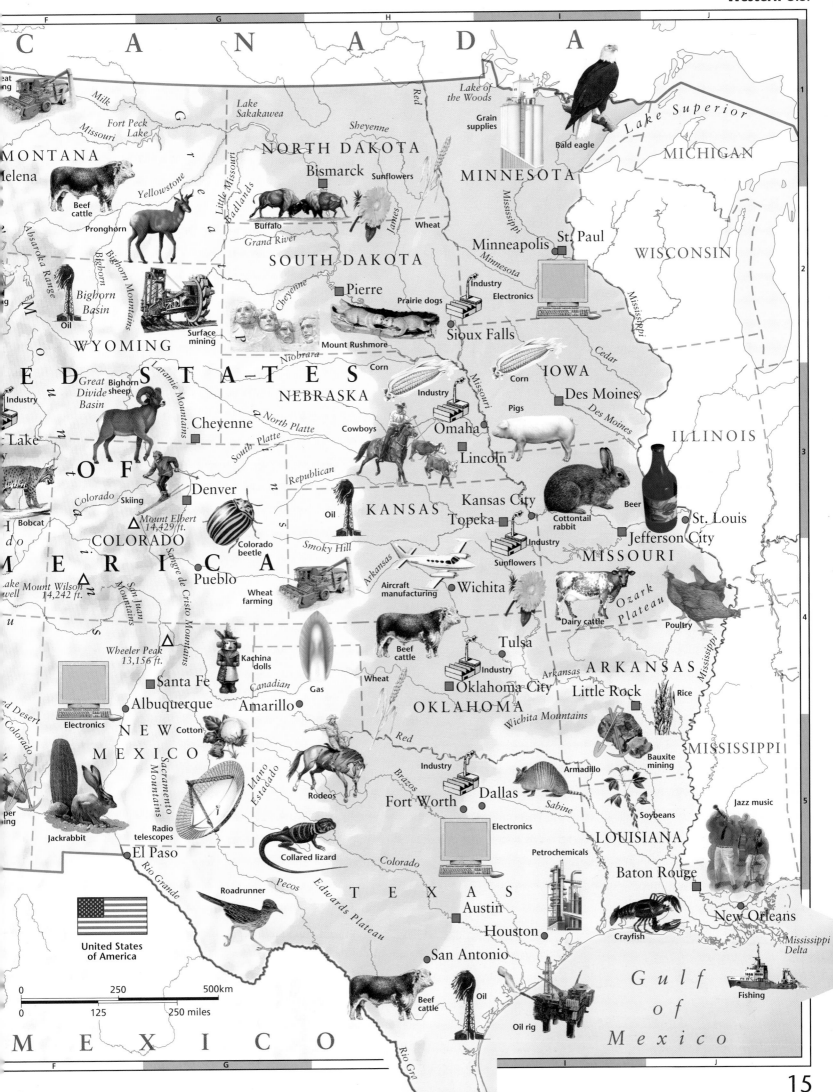

CANADA

Great
ing

MONTANA
Helena

Beef
cattle

Pronghorn

Milk
Missouri

Fort Peck
Lake

Yellowstone

Absaroka Range

Bighorn
Mountains

Bighorn

Bighorn
Basin

Oil

Surface
mining

WYOMING

Great
Divide
Basin

Bighorn
sheep

Laramie Mountains

Cheyenne

Skiing

Denver

Mount Elbert
14,429 ft.

COLORADO

Colorado
beetle

Pueblo

Mount Wilson
14,242 ft.

San Juan Mountains

Sangre de Cristo Mountains

Wheeler Peak
13,156 ft.

Kachina
dolls

Santa Fe

Albuquerque

Electronics

NEW

MEXICO

Cotton

Sacramento Mountains

Radio
telescopes

Jackrabbit

El Paso

Lake
Sakakawea

Little Missouri

Badlands

NORTH DAKOTA
Bismarck

Sunflowers

Buffalo

Grand River

Wheat

SOUTH DAKOTA

Cheyenne

Pierre

Prairie dogs

Mount Rushmore

Niobrara

STATES

NEBRASKA

North Platte

South Platte

Republican

Smoky Hill

Oil

KANSAS

Topeka

Wheat
farming

Arkansas

Aircraft
manufacturing

Wheat

OF

A

Pecos

Roadrunner

United States
of America

0   250   500km

0   125   250 miles

Llano Estacado

Edwards Plateau

Collared lizard

Colorado

TEXAS

Austin

San Antonio

Beef
cattle

Oil

Sheyenne

Red

Lake of
the Woods

Grain
supplies

Bald eagle

MINNESOTA

Minneapolis

St. Paul

Industry

Electronics

Sioux Falls

Corn

Industry

Cowboys

Omaha

Lincoln

Kansas City

Industry

Cottontail
rabbit

Sunflowers

Wichita

Beef
cattle

Tulsa

Industry

Oklahoma City

OKLAHOMA

Wichita Mountains

Red

Industry

Fort Worth

Dallas

Electronics

Petrochemicals

Houston

Oil rig

MICHIGAN

Lake Superior

WISCONSIN

Mississippi

Corn

IOWA

Des Moines

Pigs

ILLINOIS

Cedar

Des Moines

Beer

St. Louis

Jefferson City

MISSOURI

Dairy cattle

Ozark
Plateau

Poultry

Mississippi

ARKANSAS

Arkansas

Little Rock

Rice

Bauxite
mining

MISSISSIPPI

Armadillo

Sabine

Soybeans

Jazz music

LOUISIANA

Baton Rouge

New Orleans

Crayfish

Mississippi
Delta

Fishing

Gulf
of
Mexico

Rio Grande

MEXICO

Milk

Brazos

Gas

Amarillo

Rodeos

Industry

Minnesota

Mississippi

Missouri

Niobrara

15

Eastern United States

The eastern parts of the U.S. were home to the first European settlers, who arrived in America in the 1600s, and they remain the most densely populated areas today.

They contain major cities such as New York City, Chicago, and Washington, D.C. Stretching from the rocky shores of Maine down to the sunny islands of the Florida Keys, the eastern seaboard (coast) has a varied landscape with many bays and inlets. Farther inland the Appalachian mountain system, which is rich in mineral deposits, cuts through the country. Much of the surrounding area is still covered in trees—in West Virginia, for example, 75 percent of the land is forests. The states surrounding the Gulf of Mexico enjoy a mostly temperate climate. Florida is warm all year-round. It is popular with tourists from the U.S. and around the world, and it is also home to the Kennedy Space Center at Cape Canaveral.

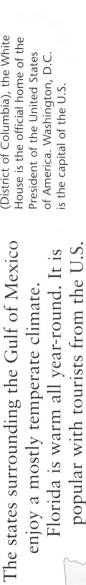

The White House
Situated in Washington, D.C. (District of Columbia), the White House is the official home of the President of the United States of America. Washington, D.C. is the capital of the U.S.

MINNESOTA

Lake Superior

Pine forests

Mining

WISCONSIN

Mississippi

Cheese

Dairy cattle

Madison

Sears Tower

Beer

Milwaukee

Lake Michigan

Chicago

Beef cattle

Machinery

IOWA

Lake Huron

Georgian Bay

Robin

Cherries

MICHIGAN

Car manufacturing

Lansing

Detroit

Toledo

Lake Erie

Cleveland

Industry

CANADA

Lake Ontario

Niagara Falls

Buffalo

PENNSYLVANIA

Glass making

Harrisburg

Dairy cattle

Machinery

New York

Apples

Electronics

NEW YORK

Albany

Catskill Mountains

Adirondack Mountains

Maple tree

Montpelier

Apples

VERMONT

Cranberries

Electronics

NEW HAMPSHIRE

Concord

Mount Washington 6,288 ft.

White Mountains

△

MASSACHUSETTS

Hartford

Machinery

CONNECTICUT

Boston

Providence

RHODE ISLAND

Martha's Vineyard

Long Island

The Statue of Liberty

Electronics

MAINE

Augusta

Paper making

Logging

Gulf of Maine

Lobster

Cape Cod

Nantucket Island

Fishing

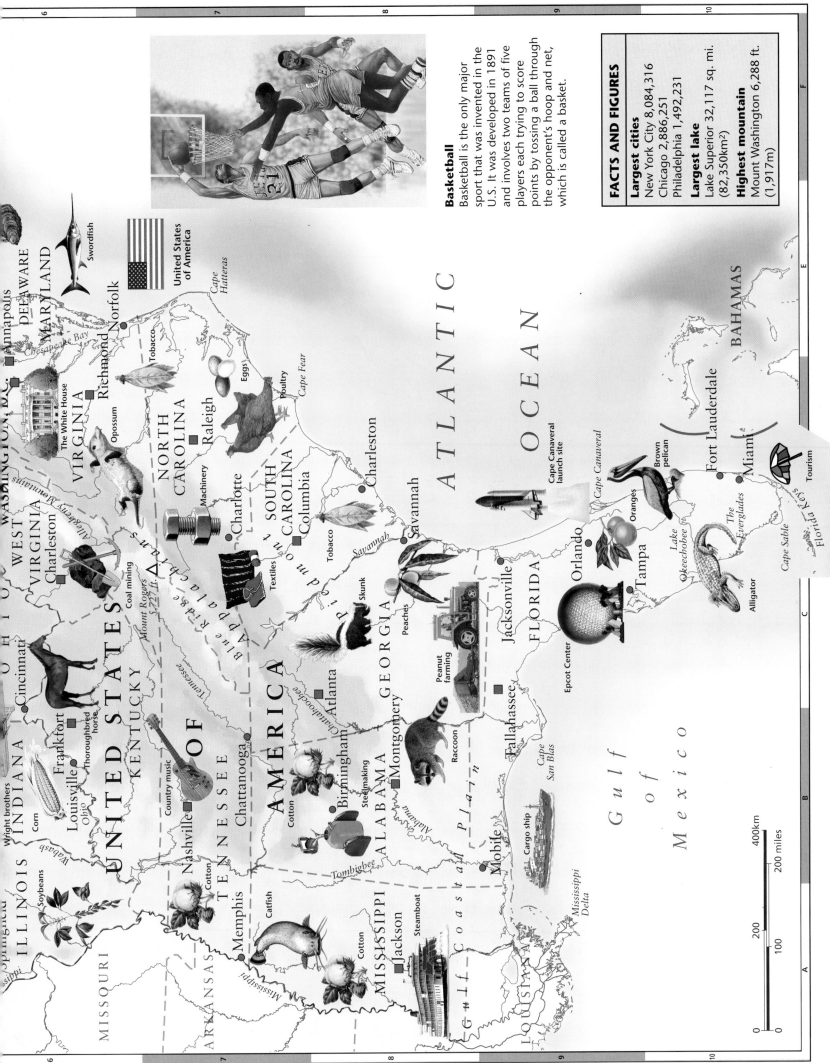

Basketball

Basketball is the only major sport that was invented in the U.S. It was developed in 1891 and involves two teams of five players each trying to score points by tossing a ball through the opponent's hoop and net, which is called a basket.

United States of America

Swordfish

FACTS AND FIGURES

Largest cities
New York City 8,084,316
Chicago 2,886,251
Philadelphia 1,492,231

Largest lake
Lake Superior 32,117 sq. mi. (82,350km²)

Highest mountain
Mount Washington 6,288 ft. (1,917m)

MISSOURI

ILLINOIS

INDIANA

Springfield

Soybeans

Corn

Wright brothers

Wabash

OHIO

Cincinnati

Thoroughbred horse

KENTUCKY

Frankfort

Louisville

Ohio

WEST VIRGINIA

Charleston

Allegheny Mountains

Coal mining

Mount Rogers 5,727 ft.

Blue Ridge

Appalachian Mountains

VIRGINIA

Opossum

Richmond

WASHINGTON, D.C.

The White House

Annapolis

DELAWARE

MARYLAND

Chesapeake Bay

Norfolk

Tobacco

NORTH CAROLINA

Raleigh

Eggs

Poultry

Cape Hatteras

Cape Fear

Machinery

Charlotte

SOUTH CAROLINA

Columbia

Charleston

Textiles

Tobacco

UNITED STATES

ARKANSAS

TENNESSEE

Nashville

Chattanooga

Memphis

Cotton

Country music

Tennessee

Catfish

Steamboat

MISSISSIPPI

Jackson

Cotton

OF

AMERICA

GEORGIA

Atlanta

Chattahoochee

Peaches

Skunk

Savannah

Savannah

ATLANTIC

OCEAN

ALABAMA

Birmingham

Montgomery

Steelmaking

Cotton

Alabama

Tombigbee

Raccoon

Peanut farming

Coastal Plain

Cape San Blas

Mobile

Cargo ship

Mississippi Delta

Mississippi

LOUISIANA

Gulf

of

Mexico

Tallahassee

Jacksonville

FLORIDA

Epcot Center

Orlando

Cape Canaveral launch site

Cape Canaveral

Tampa

Oranges

Brown pelican

Lake Okeechobee

The Everglades

Alligator

Cape Sable

Fort Lauderdale

Miami

Florida Keys

Tourism

BAHAMAS

0   200
0   100   200 miles
0   400km

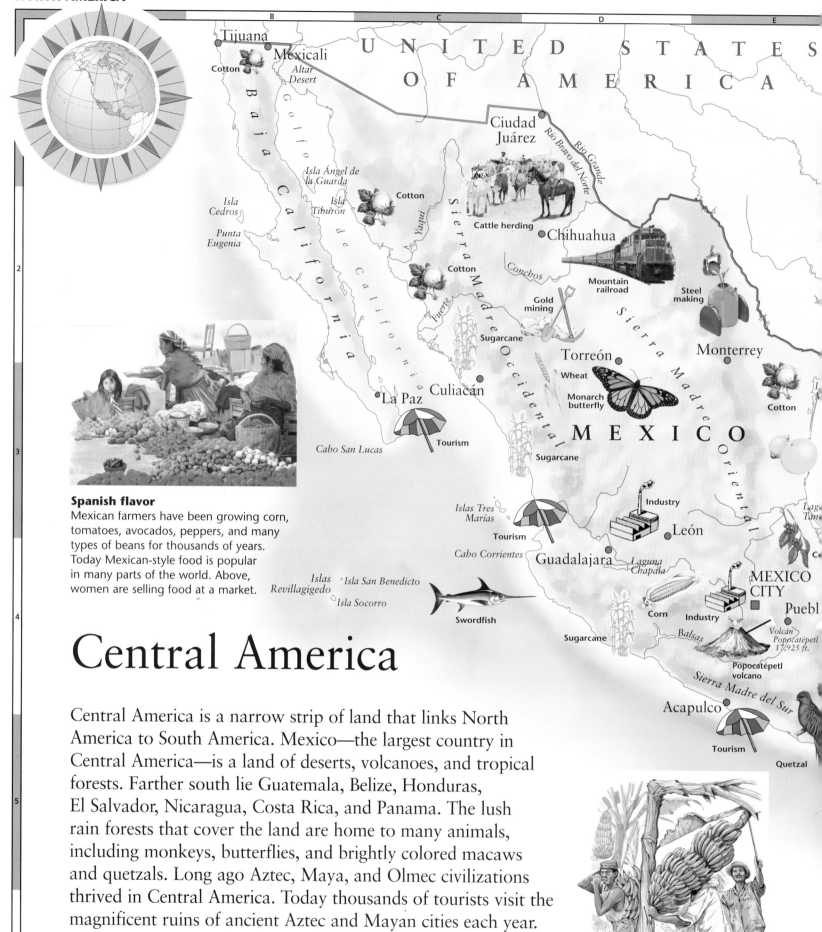

U N I T E D   S T A T E S
O F   A M E R I C A

Tijuana
Cotton
Mexicali
*Altar
Desert*

Baja California

Golfo de California

*Isla Ángel de
la Guarda*

*Isla
Cedros*

*Isla
Tiburón*

*Punta
Eugenia*

Ciudad
Juárez

Río Bravo del Norte

Río Grande

Cotton

Cattle herding

Chihuahua

Conchos

Mountain
railroad

Cotton

Yaqui

Sierra Madre Occidental

Fuerte

Gold
mining

Sugarcane

Steel
making

Sierra Madre Oriental

Monterrey

Torreón

Wheat

Monarch
butterfly

Cotton

La Paz

Culiacán

Tourism

Cabo San Lucas

M E X I C O

Sugarcane

Spanish flavor
Mexican farmers have been growing corn,
tomatoes, avocados, peppers, and many
types of beans for thousands of years.
Today Mexican-style food is popular
in many parts of the world. Above,
women are selling food at a market.

*Islas Tres
Marías*

Tourism

Cabo Corrientes

*Islas
Revillagigedo*

Isla San Benedicto

Isla Socorro

Swordfish

Industry

León

Guadalajara

*Laguna
Chapala*

Corn

Industry

MEXICO
CITY

Pueb

Puebl

*Lagu
Tam*

C

Cotton

Industry

Sugarcane

Balsas

*Volcán
Popocatépetl
17,925 ft.*

Popocatépetl
volcano

Acapulco

Sierra Madre del Sur

Tourism

Quetzal

Central America

Central America is a narrow strip of land that links North
America to South America. Mexico—the largest country in
Central America—is a land of deserts, volcanoes, and tropical
forests. Farther south lie Guatemala, Belize, Honduras,
El Salvador, Nicaragua, Costa Rica, and Panama. The lush
rain forests that cover the land are home to many animals,
including monkeys, butterflies, and brightly colored macaws
and quetzals. Long ago Aztec, Maya, and Olmec civilizations
thrived in Central America. Today thousands of tourists visit the
magnificent ruins of ancient Aztec and Mayan cities each year.

The Panama Canal—the busiest big-ship canal in the world—
is in Panama. It is 51 mi. (82km) long and links the Pacific and
Atlantic oceans. Before it opened in 1914, ships had to travel all
the way around South America in order to reach the other ocean.

Going bananas
Bananas are the main crop in
Honduras. They account for almost
one fourth of the country's income.

Bustling city

Mexico City is the third-largest city in the world and home to over 18 million inhabitants. People enjoy watching bullfighting or sports, such as baseball or soccer, at these large stadiums.

FACTS AND FIGURES

Largest cities
Mexico City 18,268,000
Guadalajara 3,847,000
Monterrey 3,468,000

Longest river
Rio Grande 2,048 mi. (3,304km)

Largest lake
Laguna de Nicaragua, 3,198 sq. mi. (8,200km²)

Highest mountain
Volcán Pico de Orizaba 18,696 ft. (5,700m)

Temples in the jungle

The Mayan people lived in Tikal, Guatemala, more than 3,000 years ago. There are more than 3,000 ruined buildings at this site, including impressive temples.

Tuna

Gulf of Mexico

Lobster

Mexico

Bay of Campeche

Oil rig

Mérida

Chichén Itzá

Isla Cozumel

Yucatan Channel

Península de Yucatan

Laguna de Términos

Scarlet macaw

Belize

BELIZE

BELMOPAN

El Petén

tmo de uantepec

Coffee

Tikal

Usumacinta

Presa de la Angostura

GUATEMALA

Sierra Madre

Volcán de Tajamulco 13,816 ft.

Coffee

Golfo de ehuantepec

GUATEMALA CITY

SAN SALVADOR

EL SALVADOR

Guatemala

El Salvador

Golfo de Honduras

HONDURAS

Coffee

Coffee

TEGUCIGALPA

Citrus fruits

Laguna de Caratasca

Patuca

Coco

Swan Islands (to Honduras)

Honduras

Bananas

Coffee

Costa de Mosquito

Nicaragua

NICARAGUA

MANAGUA

Laguna de Nicaragua

San Juan

Panama

Owl monkey

Golfo de Darién

Panama Canal

COSTA RICA

SAN JOSÉ

Coffee

Costa Rica

Golfo de los Mosquitos

PANAMA

PANAMA CITY

Golfo de Panamá

Golfo de Chiriquí

Coiba

Keel-billed toucan

COLOMBIA

| 0 | 300 | 600km |
| 0 | 150 | 300 miles |

UNITED STATES OF AMERICA (FLORIDA)

Gulf of Mexico

Tourism

Grand Bahama Freeport

Great Abaco

Bahamas

NASSAU

Eleuthera

New Providence

Cat Island

BAHAMAS

Andros Island

Straits of Florida

Cuba

HAVANA

Long Island

Yucatan Channel

Tobacco

Cigar making

CUBA

Fishing

Acklins Island

Isla de la Juventud

G

Sugarcane

•Camagüey

Scuba diving

r

e

a

Cutting sugarcane

Cayman Islands (to U.K.)

t

Santiago de Cuba

Grand Cayman

e

Tourism

r

Navassa Island (to U.S.)

Montego Bay

JAMAICA

Bananas

Mining

KINGSTON

Cruise ship

Jamaica

Party time!
Festivals and carnivals are a time to have fun. People wear colorful costumes and play music as they parade through the streets.

The Caribbean

A string of islands separates the Atlantic Ocean from the Caribbean Sea. There are many different countries in the Caribbean, as well as hundreds of islands. Cuba is the largest island, stretching more than 682 mi. (1,100km) in length. Haiti and the Dominican Republic share ownership of the second-biggest island, Hispaniola. Some of the other islands are so small that no one lives on them. All of the islands enjoy a tropical climate with a rainy season between June and November. Occasionally violent storms—called hurricanes— sweep through the Caribbean. The strong winds and torrential rain can cause serious damage. Coral reefs surround many of the islands, and tourists can scuba dive in the warm waters or explore the islands' many beautiful palm-fringed beaches.

FACTS AND FIGURES

Largest cities
Santo Domingo 2,629,000
Havana 2,268,000
Port-au-Prince 1,838,000

Highest point
Pico Duarte 10,414 ft. (3,175m)

Number of islands
More than 100

Number of hurricanes
6 per year is average in the hurricane season between June and November, with winds reaching up to 155mph (250km/h)

Beach paradise
Tourists flock to the Caribbean to enjoy the white, sandy beaches. The money that they spend there is vital for the countries' economies.

Turks & Caicos Islands
(to U.K.)

Great Inagua

A T L A N T I C   O C E A N

West Indies

Port-de-Paix

DOMINICAN
REPUBLIC

Santiago

Pico Duarte
10,414 ft

HAITI

Hispaniola

Leeward Islands

Puerto Rico
(to U.S.)

British
Virgin Islands
(to U.K.)

Anguilla
(to U.K.)

St. Martin
(to France & Netherlands)

Saint-Barthélémy (to France)

Cocoa

Mona Passage

San Juan

Virgin
Islands
(to U.S.)

Netherlands
Antilles
(to Netherlands)

Barbuda

PORT-AU-
PRINCE

SANTO
DOMINGO

St. Kitts

Nevis

ANTIGUA & BARBUDA

BASSETERRE

ST. JOHN'S

ST. KITTS
& NEVIS

Antigua

Guadeloupe Passage

Grande-Terre

Montserrat
(to U.K.)

Guadeloupe
(to France)

Basse-Terre

Antilles

Haiti

Dominican Republic

St. Kitts & Nevis

Antigua &
Barbuda

Basse-Terre

DOMINICA ROSEAU

C a r i b b e a n   S e a

Dominica

Martinique Passage

Martinique
(to France)

Barbados

Shark

Fort-de-France

ST. LUCIA

St. Lucia

Sailing

CASTRIES

St. Vincent Passage

BARBADOS

KINGSTOWN

St. Vincent

BRIDGETOWN

L e s s e r

ST. VINCENT &
THE GRENADINES

The Grenadines

Aruba
(to Netherlands)

Netherlands Antilles
(to Netherlands)

ST. GEORGE'S

St. Vincent &
the Grenadines

Oranjestad

Bonaire

GRENADA

Windward Islands

Tourism

Willemstad

Curaçao

COLOMBIA

Grenada

Tobago

0   250   500km

0   125   250 miles

PORT-OF-SPAIN

TRINIDAD
& TOBAGO

Trinidad & Tobago

Trinidad

V E N E Z U E L A

Aruba
(to Netherlands)   Netherlands Antilles
(to Netherlands)   GRENADA

CARACAS   TRINIDAD & TOBAGO

VENEZUELA   GEORGETOWN
GUYANA   PARAMARIBO

BOGOTÁ   Cayenne

COLOMBIA   SURINAME   French
Guiana
(to France)

QUITO

ECUADOR

P E R U   B R A Z I L

LIMA

B O L I V I A   BRASÍLIA

LA PAZ

SUCRE

PARAGUAY

Islas de los
Desventurados
(to Chile)   ASUNCIÓN

Juan Fernández
Island
(to Chile)   URUGUAY

SANTIAGO   BUENOS AIRES   MONTEVIDEO

A R G E N T I N A

C
H
I
L
E

| 0 | 500 | 1000km |
| 0 | 250 | 500 miles |

Falkland Islands
(Islas Malvinas)
(to U.K.)

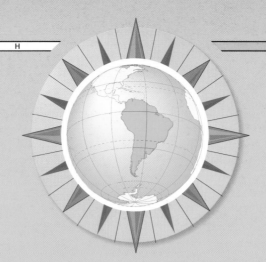

Mighty river
The enormous Amazon river flows across South America and supports a huge variety of life. These giant lily pads thrive in a section of slow-moving water.

SOUTH AMERICA

South America is the fourth-largest continent. It stretches from the Caribbean Sea in the north to the icy lands at its southern tip. In the northeast of the continent lies the tropical Amazon Basin, where it is hot and wet all year-round. The mighty Amazon river and Amazon rain forest—the world's largest rain forest—are found there. Farther south the climate is cooler, and there are large open plains. The longest range of mountains in the world, the Andes, extends for 4,495 mi. (7,250km) along the western edge of the continent.

Most South American countries are Spanish speaking, and most of the continent's people live in large cities along the coast.

Rugged mountains
The Torres del Paine National Park is in the far south of Chile. Its unspoiled scenery shows the lakes and mountains at their most beautiful.

Haunting music
A young Peruvian girl plays a traditional tune on the rondador, or panpipes. The music is made by blowing across the top of hollow bamboo tubes.

Northern South America

The largest tropical rain forest in the world stretches across northern South America, filling the Amazon Basin. This densely forested region is full of valuable resources, including cacao for chocolate, nuts, rare hardwoods, and plants that can be used to make medicines. But humans are rapidly destroying the rain forests by cutting down the trees for timber and to search for valuable minerals, as well as clearing the land for agriculture.

Brazil is the largest country in South America and covers almost one half of the continent. Much of the world's coffee and sugarcane is grown there. Most of its people live in towns and cities close to the coast. Brazil has a very young population—almost half the people are younger than 20 years old. Venezuela is the richest country in South America because it has huge oil reserves and other minerals. It also has the world's highest waterfall, Angel Falls.

The countries on the western side of the continent are dominated by the Andes mountains—the longest mountain range in the world. Bolivia has two capitals—La Paz and Sucre. La Paz, the seat of government, high up in the Andes, is the world's highest capital city.

Standing tall
The magnificent statue of Christ the Redeemer towers over Rio de Janeiro, Brazil's cultural capital—playground of the rich and bustling Atlantic port.

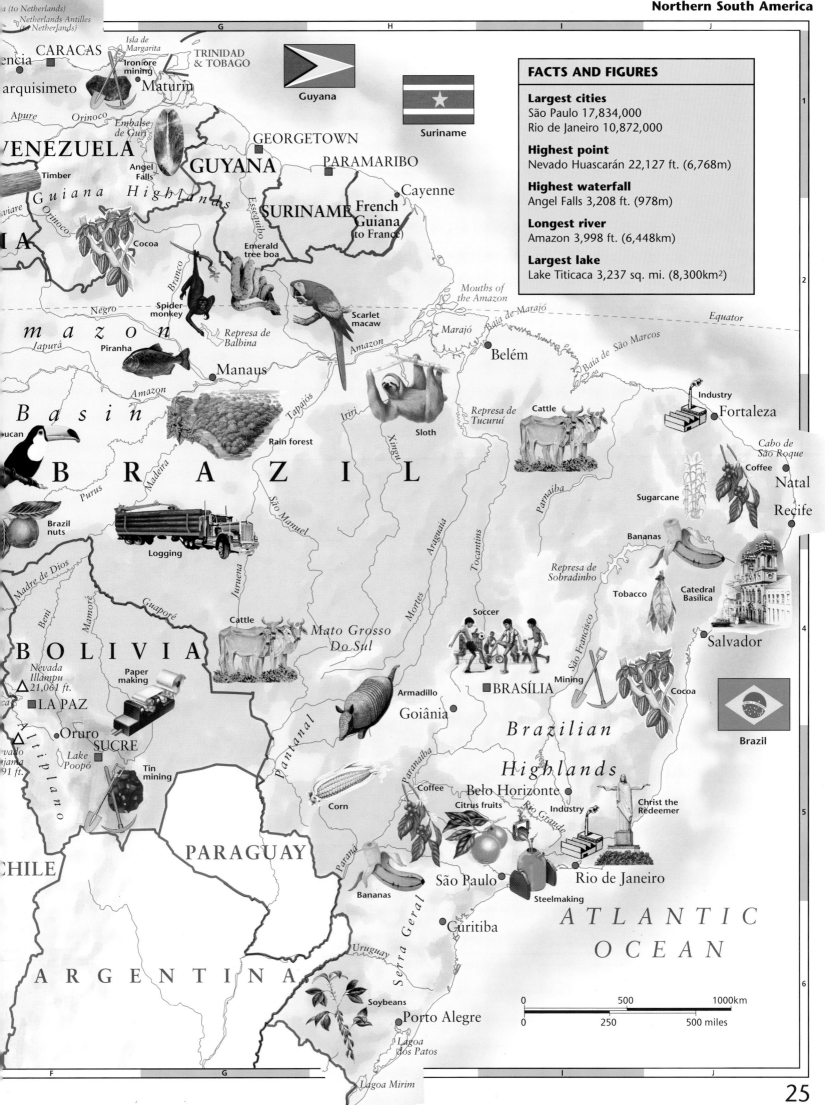

a (to Netherlands)
Netherlands Antilles
(to Netherlands)

CARACAS
Isla de
Margarita
Iron ore
mining
Maturín
TRINIDAD & TOBAGO
Guyana
Suriname

encia
arquisimeto

VENEZUELA
Apure
Orinoco
Embalse
de Guri

GEORGETOWN
PARAMARIBO
Cayenne

GUYANA
SURINAME
French Guiana
(to France)

Angel
Falls
Timber
Guiana Highlands
Cocoa

IA
Orinoco
viare

FACTS AND FIGURES

Largest cities
São Paulo 17,834,000
Rio de Janeiro 10,872,000

Highest point
Nevado Huascarán 22,127 ft. (6,768m)

Highest waterfall
Angel Falls 3,208 ft. (978m)

Longest river
Amazon 3,998 ft. (6,448km)

Largest lake
Lake Titicaca 3,237 sq. mi. (8,300km²)

Branco
Negro
Essequibo
Emerald
tree boa
Scarlet
macaw

*Mouths of
the Amazon*
Marajó
Baía de Marajó
Equator

a m a z o n
Japurá
Piranha
Spider
monkey
*Represa de
Balbina*
Amazon

Baía de São Marcos
Belém

ucan
B a s i n
Manaus
Amazon
Tapajós
Iriri
Xingu
Sloth
Rain forest
Cattle
*Represa de
Tucuruí*
Industry
Fortaleza

B R A Z I L
*Cabo de
São Roque*
Coffee
Natal
Recife

Purus
Madeira
São Manuel
Parnaiba
Sugarcane

Brazil
nuts
Logging
Bananas

Madre de Dios
Ituruena
Mortes
Araguaia
Tocantins
*Represa de
Sobradinho*
Tobacco
Catedral
Basílica

Beni
Mamoré
Guaporé
Cattle
*Mato Grosso
Do Sul*
Soccer
São Francisco
Mining
Cocoa

B O L I V I A
Nevada
Illampu
21,061 ft.
Paper
making
Armadillo
BRASÍLIA
Salvador

ca
LA PAZ
Goiânia
Brazilian
Brazil

vado
jama
91 ft.
Oruro
SUCRE
Lake
Poopó
Tin
mining
Pantanal
H i g h l a n d s
Belo Horizonte
Christ the
Redeemer

Altiplano
Corn
Paranaíba
Coffee
Citrus fruits
Rio Grande
Industry

CHILE
PARAGUAY
Paraná
Bananas
São Paulo
Steelmaking
Rio de Janeiro

Corn

Serra Geral
Curitiba
**A T L A N T I C
O C E A N**

A R G E N T I N A
Uruguay
Soybeans
Porto Alegre

0   500   1000km
0   250   500 miles

*Lagoa
dos Patos*

Lagoa Mirim

25

Southern South America

Four countries make up southern South America. They are Chile, Argentina, Paraguay, and Uruguay. The Falkland Islands in the Atlantic Ocean are British territories. Chile is a long, thin country sandwiched between the ocean and the high Andes mountains. The driest place in the world—the Atacama desert—is in Chile.

Argentina has a varied landscape, including the jagged peaks of the Andes and the vast, flat grasslands of the Pampas region. In the south of the country is Patagonia, a bleak plateau. At the tip of southern South America lies the remote and bitterly cold island of Tierra del Fuego, only 620 mi. (1,000km) away from Antarctica.

Uruguay and Argentina share the estuary to the Rio de la Plata, which is a large trading route to the middle of the continent. Paraguay is a landlocked country, which means it has no coasts. Most of the people there are of mixed Native American and Spanish descent. In the other countries many of the people are descendants from European settlers, who arrived around 400 years ago.

PERU

BOLIVIA

BRAZIL

Paraguay

PARAGUAY

Pilcomayo

Pantheon of Heroes

ASUNCIÓN

Hydroelectricity

Paraná

Paraguay

Posadas

Uruguay

URUGUAY

Uruguay

Lagoa Mirim

Cattle

Sheep

Cattle

Cotton

Resistencia

Paraná

Santa Fé

Rosario

La

Soybeans

Tobacco

Timber

Gran Chaco

Giant anteater

Burrowing owl

Laguna Mar Chiquita

Soccer

Córdoba

Rhea

Gaucho

Tobacco

Ovenbird

Salado

Santiago del Estero

Textiles

Wine making

San Miguel de Tucumán

Ojos del Salado Nevado 22,609 ft.

A

L

E

Cavy

Wine making

Mendoza

SANTIAGO

Aconcagua 22,831 ft.

Valparaíso

Copper mining

Antofagasta

Atacama Desert

Andean condor

26

Mar del Plata

Dolphin

Cattle

Fishing

Gauchos

Skilled herders on horseback—called gauchos—take care of their cattle in Argentina. The country's vast plains provide good land for cattle and sheep farming.

Punta Norte

Bahía Blanca

Mara

Bahía Blanca

Punta Rasa

Río Negro

Golfo San Matías

Península Valdés 131 ft.

Right whale

Argentina

Salado

Maned wolf

Colorado

Grapes

Armadillo

Paper making

Concepción

Fishing

Salmon

Isla Grande de Chiloé

Chubut

Chico

Deseado

Cabo Tres Puntas

Golfo San Jorge

Corcovado

Golfo Corcovado

Los Chones Archipelago

Península de Taitao

Golfo de Penas

Timber

Isla Wellington

Santa Cruz

Chico

A T L A N T I C

O C E A N

Sheep

Oil rig

Bahía Grande

Strait of Magellan

Falkland Islands (Islas Malvinas) (to U.K.)

West Falkland

East Falkland

Stanley

Rockhopper penguin

Isla de los Estados

Tierra del Fuego

Cape Horn

Reina Adelaida Archipelago

Punta Arenas

Chile

Atacama Desert

The Atacama Desert in Chile is the driest place on Earth. Some parts of this cold desert have not had any rain for more than 400 years.

FACTS AND FIGURES

Largest cities
Buenos Aires 12, 106,000
Santiago 5,551,000
Montevideo 1,329,000

Highest point
Aconcagua 22,609 ft. (6,960m)

Lowest point
Península Valdés 131 ft. (40m) below sea level

Longest river
Paraná-Rio de la Plata 3,026 mi. (4,880km)

Biggest dam
Itaipú Dam on Paraná river (most massive in world by volume of water)

Number of cattle
58 million in Argentina (2000)

600km

300 miles

300

150

0

0

Greenland
(to Denmark)

AFRICA

REYKJAVIK ICELAND

Jan Mayen Island
(to Norway)

Bjørnøya
(to Norway)

Vesterålen
Lofoten

N O R W A Y

S W E D E N

FINLAND

OSLO

HELSINKI

STOCKHOLM

TALLINN

ESTONIA

Gotland

RIGA LATVIA

Öland

LITHUANIA

RUSS. FED.

VILNIUS

R U S
F E D E

MOSCOW

MINSK

BELARUS

Faroe Islands
(to Denmark)

Shetland
Islands
(to U.K.)

Orkney
Islands

Outer Hebrides

UNITED
KINGDOM

REPUBLIC
OF IRELAND

DUBLIN

Isle of Man
(to U.K.)

DENMARK

COPENHAGEN

NETHERLANDS

AMSTERDAM

LONDON

BERLIN

WARSAW

GERMANY

POLAND

THE HAGUE

Channel Islands
(to U.K.)

BRUSSELS

BELGIUM

LUXEMBOURG

LUX.

PARIS

PRAGUE

CZECH
REPUBLIC

KIEV

UKRAINE

SLOVAKIA

VIENNA

BRATISLAVA

FRANCE

BERN

VADUZ LIECH.

AUSTRIA

BUDAPEST

MOLDOVA

CHISINĂU

SWITZ.

SLOVENIA

HUNGARY

LJUBLJANA

ZAGREB

CROATIA

ROMANIA

PORTUGAL

ANDORRA
LA VELLA ANDORRA

MONACO

SAN
MARINO

BOSNIA &
HERZEGOVINA

BELGRADE

SARAJEVO

BUCHAREST

LISBON

MADRID

SPAIN

Corsica
(to France)

ITALY

ROME

VATICAN
CITY

SERBIA &
MONTENEGRO

BULGARIA

SOFIA

SKOPJE

MACEDONIA

T U R K E Y

Majorca

Ibiza

Minorca

Balearic Islands

Sardinia
(to Italy)

TIRANA

ALBANIA

GREECE

Gibraltar
(to U.K.)

Sicily

MALTA

VALLETTA

ATHENS

Rhodes

Crete

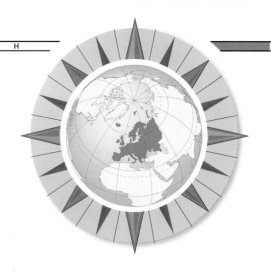

EUROPE

Europe is the second-smallest continent, but its 43 countries are heavily populated, making it the most crowded continent of all. It stretches from the lands along the Atlantic Ocean in the west to the Ural Mountains in the Russian Federation in the east and from the Baltic Sea in the north to the Mediterranean Sea in the south. It is a continent of peninsulas and islands, and its ragged coastline measures almost 37,820 mi. (61,000km). If you stretched this out, it would circle the equator more than one-and-a-half times. Much of Europe is mountainous. The countries around the Mediterranean Sea enjoy hot, dry summers and warm, wet winters. The climate in much of the rest of Europe is mild.

Many of the countries in Europe have existed for hundreds of years; others have been formed recently and are still only a few years old.

A S I A

A N

T I O N

A S I A

National traditions
Many countries have strong traditions. These girls are dressed in the national costumes of Latvia.

Rugged coastline
The Balearic Islands, shown here, are just some of the many islands and coastal regions throughout Europe that are enjoyed by tourists every year.

Northwestern Europe

Four countries in northwestern Europe make up the area called Scandinavia—Norway, Sweden, Finland, and Denmark. Far to the west of these lies the volcanic island of Iceland. The far north of Scandinavia is deep inside the Arctic Circle, but its cold climate is tempered by the North Atlantic Drift—an ocean current that carries warm water across the Atlantic Ocean.

The Scandinavian landscape is rugged, mountainous, and wooded. Along the coast of Norway are long, deep sea inlets called fjords. There are also thousands of lakes—Sweden alone has more than 95,000. Norway has five of the world's highest waterfalls—Utigardfoss, Mongefossen, Espelandsfoss, Ostra Mardolafoss, and Tyssestrengene. More than half of Sweden's land surface is covered with dense forests. Denmark's land in contrast is mostly flat, and much of it is used for farmland.

Iceland is partially covered by ice fields and glaciers. The land is volcanic and has many geysers and hot springs.

FACTS AND FIGURES

Largest cities
Stockholm 1,626,000
Copenhagen 1,332,000
Largest lake
Vänern 2,178 sq. mi.
(5,585km²)
Highest point
Galdhopiggen 8,097 ft.
(2,479m)
Highest waterfall
Utigardfoss (2,624 ft.,
800m) is the third highest
in the world

Iceland (inset map)

Iceland

ICELAND

Akureyri

Puffin

Húnaflói

Breidafjördebur

Faxaflói

Keflavík

Arctic Circle

Geyser

REYKJAVÍK

Vatnajökull

Hvannadalshnúkur
6,950 ft.

Cod

ATLANTIC
OCEAN

200km

100 miles

100

50

Main map

RUSSIAN FEDERATION

Barents Sea

Varangerfjorden

Lemming

Kirkenes

Teno

Teno

Teno

Teno

Porsangen

Lokan
Tekojärvi

Livojoki

Inarijärvi

Kemijoki

Kemi

Ounasjoki

Lapland

Sami people

Tornionjoki

Kalixälven

North
Cape

Magerøya Cape

Rolvsøya

Søroya

Seiland

Reindeer

Könkamaälven

Iron ore mining

Steel
making

Luleå

Fish processing

Ringvassøya

Kvaløya

Senja

Tromsø

Torneträsk

Kebnekaise
6,924 ft.

Kiruna

Luleälven

Lilleälven

Narvik

Andøya

Hinnøya

Austvågøya

Langøya

Vestvågøya

Pine marten

Skelleftei

Logging

Vesterålen

Moskenesøya

Lofoten

Bodø

Vestfjorden

Saltfjorden

Arctic Circle

Norwegian
Sea

Cod

Fjords

Vega

Rofsvatnet

 vasl

Norway

Famous fjords

Norway's coastline is famous for its deep sea inlets called fjords. During the last Ice Age glaciers gouged huge hollows in the land. When the ice melted and the sea level rose, these troughs filled up with water.

The British Isles

The British Isles are made up of two large islands and many smaller ones that lie off the coast of northwest Europe, surrounded by the Atlantic Ocean.

The two larger islands are Great Britain and Ireland. Great Britain consists of England, Scotland, and Wales, which together with the northern part of Ireland—called Northern Ireland—make up the United Kingdom. The rest of Ireland—the Republic of Ireland—is a separate country.

The British Isles enjoy a mild climate, which is influenced by the warm Gulf Stream. This is an ocean current that carries warm water from the Straits of Florida across the Atlantic Ocean toward western Europe, helping keep the area warm. The winters can be snowy and wet, with cold winds coming from the north or east. The summers are generally warm, although winds from the southwest can bring rain.

Much of the land is used for farming. But almost 90 percent of the population live in towns and cities.

In the 1800s many factories were built, and big cities developed to support them. Today the factories have declined, and more people work in service industries such as banking and insurance.

London's skyline
The dome of St. Paul's Cathedral stands high up above the surrounding buildings. Built by Sir Christopher Wren in 1672, the dome is one of the finest in the world.

FACTS AND FIGURES

Largest cities
London 7,640,000
Birmingham 2,373,000
Manchester 2,353,000
Glasgow 1,168,000
In A.D. 1900 London was the biggest city in the world

Largest lake
Lough Neagh 154 sq. mi. (396km²)

Longest lake
Loch Ness 22 mi. (35km)

Longest river
Shannon 161 mi. (372km)

Highest mountain
Ben Nevis 4,405 ft. (1,343m)

Total number of islands
More than 5,000

Lerwick

Fair Isle

Shetland Islands
Mainland

Gray seal

Seagull

Cod

Fishing

Oil rig

Kirkwall

Orkney Islands
Mainland
Hoy

Wick

Aberdeen

Dee

Red deer

Don

SCOTLAND

Spey
Ben Macdui
4,294 ft.

Dundee

Edinburgh Castle
Firth of Forth

Perth

Inverness
Loch Ness

Grampian Mountains

skiing

Moray Firth

Sheep

Cape Wrath

Puffin

Northwest Highlands

Ben Nevis
4,405 ft.

Fort William

Oban

The Minch

Skye

Eigg
Rum
Muck

Mull
Colonsay
Jura

Coll
Tiree

Canna

Lewis

Harris

The Little Minch

North Uist

South Uist

Barra

St. Kilda

Inner Hebrides

Outer Hebrides

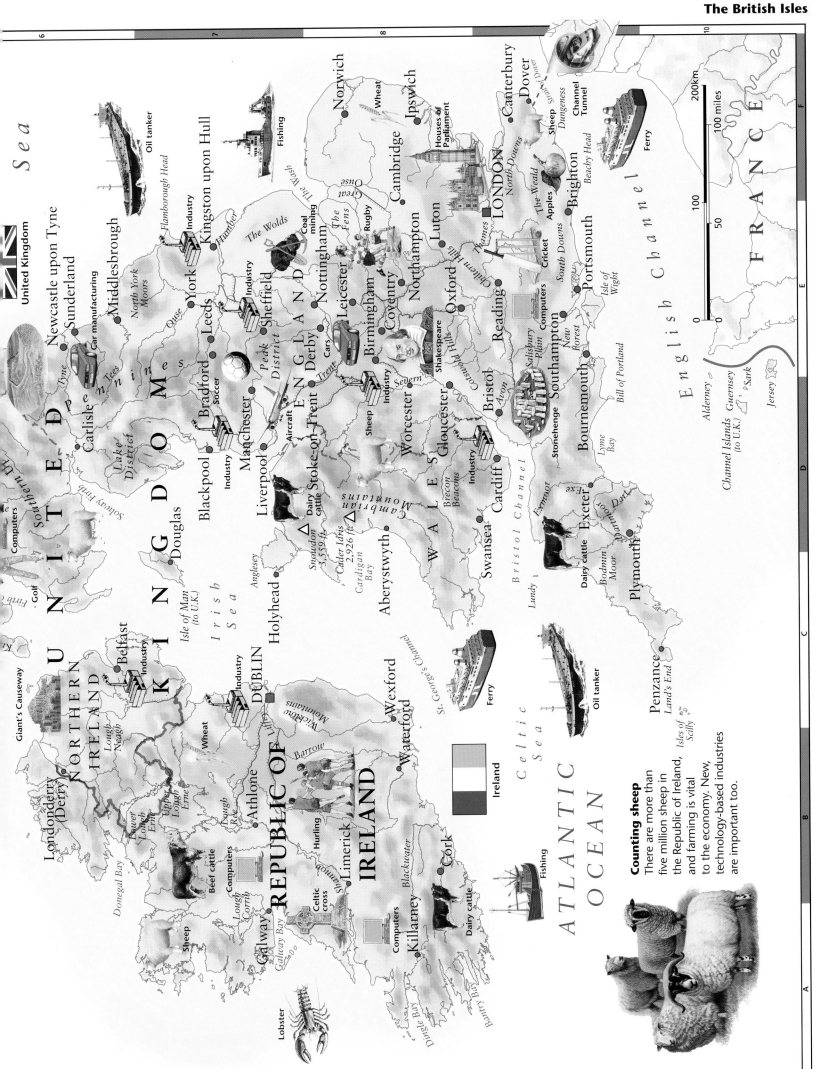

United Kingdom

N o r t h   S e a

Oil tanker
Newcastle upon Tyne
Sunderland
Car manufacturing
Middlesbrough
Flamborough Head
North York Moors
Industry
Kingston upon Hull
Fishing
York
Leeds
The Wolds
Coal mining
Industry
Sheffield
Harbour
Norwich
Wheat
Ipswich
Cambridge
The Fens
Great Ouse
Rugby
Nottingham
Leicester
Derby
Cars
Trent
Houses of Parliament
LONDON
Canterbury
Dover
Strait of Dover
Channel Tunnel
Sheep
Dungeness
North Downs
The Weald
Apples
Brighton
Beachy Head
Ferry

Carlisle
Computers
Newcastle
Solway Firth
Tyne
Tees
P e n n i n e s
Lake District
Peak District
Soccer
Bradford
Manchester
Blackpool
Industry
Liverpool
Aircraft
Stoke-on-Trent
Dairy cattle
E N G L A N D
Birmingham
Coventry
Shakespeare
Worcester
Sheep
Industry
Severn
Cotswold Hills
Gloucester
Industry
Oxford
Chiltern Hills
Northampton
Luton
Thames
Reading
Cricket
Computers
Salisbury Plain
New Forest
Southampton
Stonehenge
Portsmouth
Isle of Wight
Bournemouth
South Downs
Lyme Bay
Bill of Portland
Exmoor
Exe
Dart
Dartmoor
Exeter
Dairy cattle
Bodmin Moor
Plymouth
Lundy
Land's End
Penzance
Isles of Scilly

Douglas
Isle of Man (to U.K.)
Irish Sea
Anglesey
Snowdon 3,559 ft
Cader Idris 2,926 ft
Cambrian Mountains
W A L E S
Brecon Beacons
Industry
Cardiff
Swansea
Aberystwyth
Cardigan Bay
Bristol
Avon
Bristol Channel

U N I T E D   K I N G D O M

Giant's Causeway
Londonderry (Derry)
NORTHERN IRELAND
Belfast
Industry
Lough Neagh
Lower Lough Erne
Upper Lough Erne
Holyhead
DUBLIN
Industry
Wicklow Mountains
Wexford
Waterford
St. George's Channel

REPUBLIC OF IRELAND
Barrow
Athlone
Lough Ree
Lough Corrib
Galway
Galway Bay
Donegal Bay
Beef cattle
Computers
Wheat
Hurling
Celtic cross
Limerick
Shannon
Blackwater
Killarney
Computers
Dairy cattle
Cork
Sheep
Dingle Bay
Bantry Bay

Lobster

Fishing

Ferry

Oil tanker

ATLANTIC OCEAN
Celtic Sea

Ireland

Counting sheep
There are more than five million sheep in the Republic of Ireland, and farming is vital to the economy. New, technology-based industries are important too.

E n g l i s h   C h a n n e l
F R A N C E
Alderney
Guernsey
Channel Islands (to U.K.)
Sark
Jersey

200km
100 miles
100
50
0

Germany and the Low Countries

Belgium, the Netherlands, and Luxembourg are small countries where the land is low and flat. Because of this, they are also known as the Low Countries. Around 40 percent of the land in the Netherlands has been reclaimed from the sea. In order to hold back the water, dikes or seawalls have been built. The reclaimed land is excellent farming land, and the Netherlands is known for its agricultural goods, especially dairy products and flowers. Belgium, too, is mostly flat and also relies on dikes to hold the sea back. Much of tiny Luxembourg is rolling plateau land, and fertile farmland is found here.

Germany is a large country—the fourth-largest in Europe. The central area is made up of highlands and plateaus. The Bohemian Forest is found farther south. Even farther south are the Bavarian Alps, which border Austria. The Black Forest, in the southwest of the country, is mountainous and popular with tourists.

All four countries are prosperous, and their people enjoy a high standard of living. Belgium's capital, Brussels, contains the major offices of the European Union. Luxembourg is an important banking center. Germany was divided up into two countries, East Germany and West Germany, for 45 years before it became one country again in 1990. It is now Europe's leading industrial country.

FACTS AND FIGURES

Largest cities
Berlin 3,390,000
Brussels 1,134,000
Amsterdam 1,105,000
Highest mountain
Zugspitze 9,719 ft.
(2,963m)
Longest river
Danube 1,772 mi.
(2,858km)

Living in the cold
The climate in the higher areas of the Black Forest in Germany is raw and cold in the winter, but the valleys are mild and have good pasturelands. Winter sports are popular here. The distinctive houses are built with steeply sloping roofs so that snow will slide off of them.

Baltic Sea

Pomeranian Bay

Odehaff

Usedom

Rügen

Shipbuilding

Rostock

Beef cattle

Schweriner See

Mecklenburger Bucht

Fehmarn

Lübeck

Kieler Bucht

Industry

Kiel

Industry

Hamburg

DENMARK

Nord-Ostsee-Kanal

Dairy cattle

Sylt

North Frisian Islands

North Sea

Helgoland

Helgoländer Bucht

Frisian Islands

East Frisian Islands

Bremerhaven

France

France is the largest country in western Europe. The land is very different throughout the country. In the northeast the Vosges mountains form a border with Germany, while the Alps separate France from Italy. The southwestern border is formed by the Pyrenees, and to the west is the Atlantic Ocean. There are rugged highlands in central France, as well as many beautiful river valleys. Corsica—the fourth-largest island in the Mediterranean—belongs to France.

The climate varies across such a large area, which means that many different crops can be grown. These include wheat, corn, peaches, and grapes, which are made into some of the world's finest wines. French food is also of high quality, and French cooking is enjoyed all over the world.

Tourism plays a large part in the French economy. Every year thousands of people enjoy vacations along the warm Mediterranean coast, in the French countryside, or in the cold, snowy mountainous regions, where winter sports, such as skiing, are popular.

The tiny nation of Monaco, on the south coast near the Italian border, is the second-smallest independent country in the world.

FACTS AND FIGURES

Largest cities
Paris 9,658,000
Marseille 1,350,000
Lyon 1,349,000

Longest river
Loire 632 mi. (1,020km)

Highest mountain
Mont Blanc 15,777 ft. (4,810m). This is the second-highest mountain in Europe

Number of tourists
75 million visitors per year (2000)

Map labels

UNITED KINGDOM
English Channel
Ferry
Alderney
Cap de la Hague
Channel Islands (to U.K.)
Guernsey
Jersey
Le Ha...
Caen
Golfo de Saint-Malo
Industry
Tourism
Brest
Île d'Ouessant
Fruits and vegetables
Iron ore mining
Pointe du Raz
Quimperlé
Standing stones at Carnac
Rennes
Le Ma...
Lorient
Computers
Saumu... Castle
Pointe de Penmarch
Angers
Belle-Île
Loire
St.-Nazaire
Nantes
Île de Noirmoutier
Wine making
F
Poit...
ATLANTIC
OCEAN
Île de Ré
La Rochelle
Île d'Oléron
Charente
Angoulê...
Bay of Biscay
Water sports
Gironde
Industry
Cap Ferret
Bordeaux
G...
Peaches
Tourism
Gulf of Gascony
Adour
Bayonne
Gas
Pau
Lourdes
Vigne 10,8...
SPAIN
France

High-speed travel
TGVs can travel at speeds of 186mph. TGV stands for *le train à grande vitesse*, which means "high-speed train."

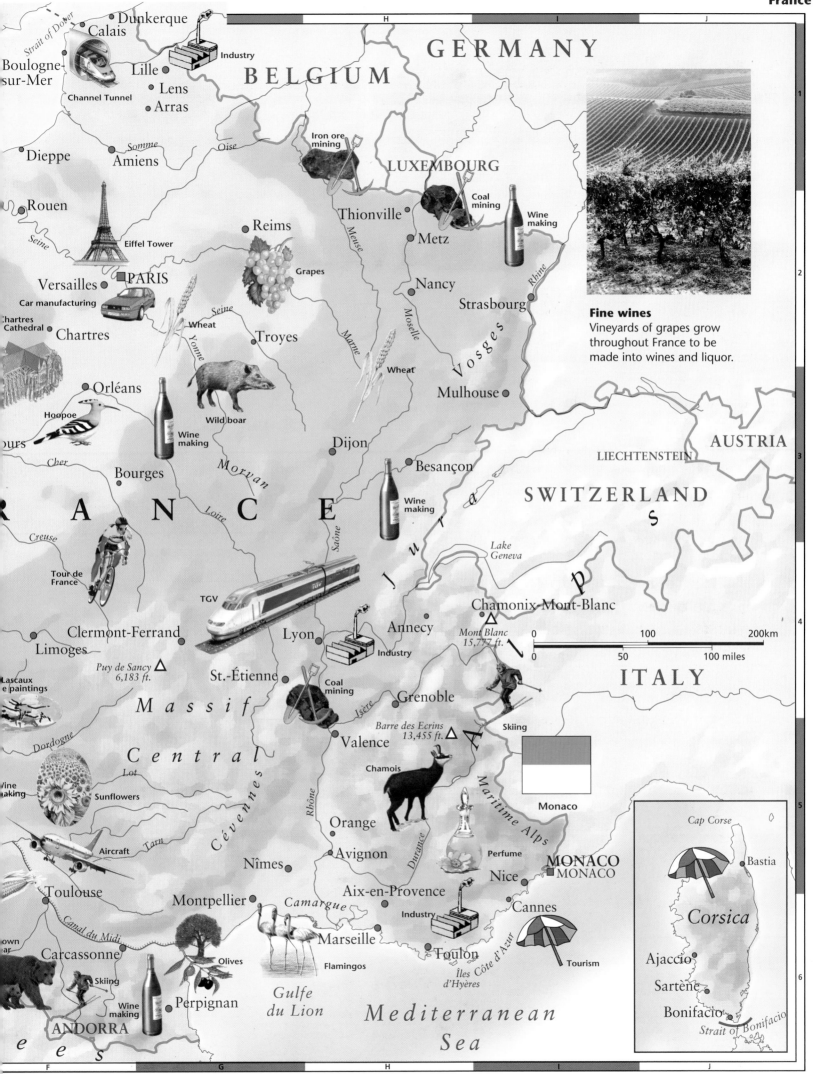

GERMANY

BELGIUM

LUXEMBOURG

Strait of Dover

Boulogne-sur-Mer

Calais

Dunkerque

Lille

Lens

Arras

Channel Tunnel

Dieppe

Somme

Amiens

Oise

Iron ore mining

Thionville

Meuse

Coal mining

Metz

Wine making

Rouen

Seine

Eiffel Tower

Reims

Grapes

Nancy

Rhine

Strasbourg

Fine wines
Vineyards of grapes grow throughout France to be made into wines and liquor.

Versailles

PARIS

Car manufacturing

Chartres Cathedral

Chartres

Wheat

Seine

Yonne

Troyes

Marne

Moselle

Wheat

Vosges

Mulhouse

Orléans

Hoopoe

ours

Wine making

Wild boar

Dijon

Besançon

AUSTRIA

LIECHTENSTEIN

SWITZERLAND

Cher

Bourges

Morvan

Loire

Wine making

Jura

Saône

Lake Geneva

Creuse

Tour de France

TGV

A
l
p
s

Clermont-Ferrand

Puy de Sancy 6,183 ft.

Limoges

Lyon

Annecy

Mont Blanc 15,777 ft.

Chamonix-Mont-Blanc

0   100   200km

0   50   100 miles

Lascaux cave paintings

St.-Étienne

Industry

Coal mining

Isère

Grenoble

ITALY

Massif

Barre des Ecrins 13,455 ft.

Skiing

Dordogne

Central

Valence

Lot

Chamois

Maritime Alps

Wine making

Sunflowers

Cévennes

Tarn

Rhône

Orange

Durance

Perfume

Monaco

Aircraft

Nîmes

Avignon

Aix-en-Provence

MONACO
MONACO

Nice

Cap Corse

Bastia

Toulouse

Montpellier

Camargue

Industry

Cannes

Corsica

Canal du Midi

Olives

Marseille

Toulon

Tourism

Îles Côte d'Azur d'Hyères

Ajaccio

own

Carcassonne

Skiing

Flamingos

Sartène

bear

Wine making

Perpignan

Gulfe du Lion

Bonifacio

ANDORRA

Mediterranean Sea

Strait of Bonifacio

e   e   s

Spain and Portugal

The countries of Spain, Portugal, and tiny Andorra make up the Iberian Peninsula—a landmass that juts out from southern Europe. It has a varied landscape, with mountains called sierras and a broad central plateau. The lands along the northern and western coasts are fertile farming regions and benefit from Atlantic rains. Madrid, in the heart of Spain, bakes under the hot summer sun but has cold winters. It is the capital of Spain and is a lively and bustling city.

Farther south on the Mediterranean coast the climate is hotter, making the region popular with tourists. The climate along the coasts of Portugal is cooler, with warm summers and milder winters.

Andorra is a tiny country high up in the Pyrenees. The winters there can be harsh, with lots of snow, but the summers are sunny and dry.

Gibraltar is a tiny British colony linked to Spain by a narrow strip of land only 2 mi. (3km) long.

FACTS AND FIGURES

Largest cities
Madrid 3,969,000
Barcelona 3,300,000
Lisbon 2,900,000

Longest river
Tagus 624 mi. (1,007km)

Highest mountain
Mulhacén 11,411 ft. (3,478m)

Highest capital
Andorra La Vella is the highest capital city in Europe

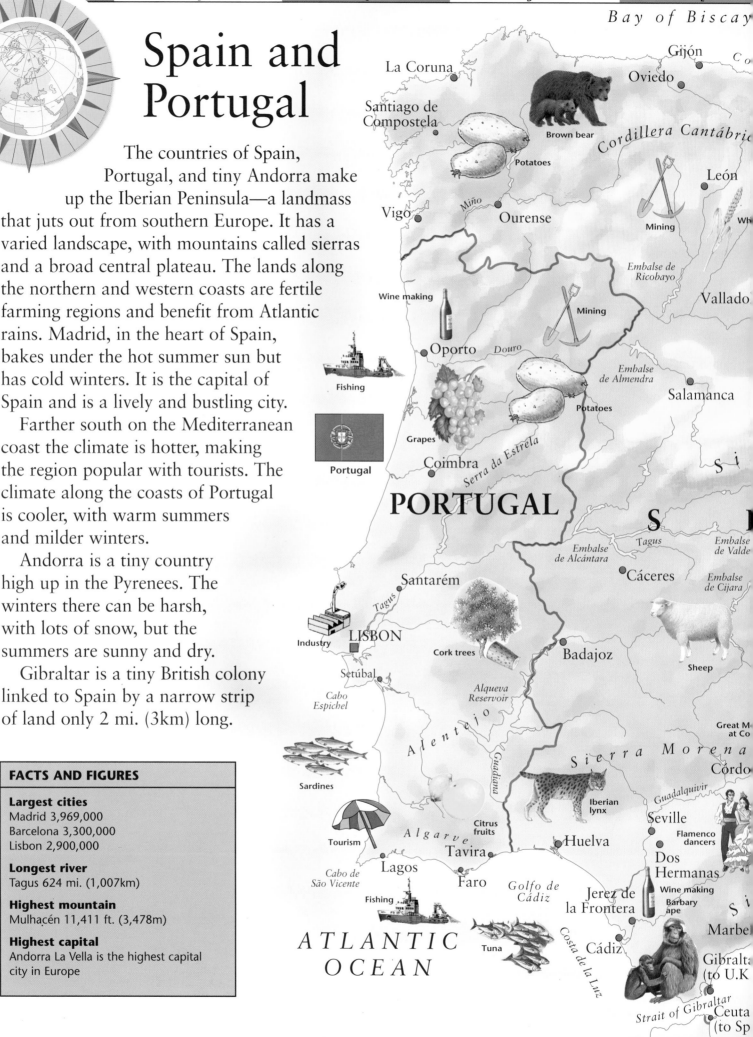

Bay of Biscay

Gijón
Oviedo
La Coruna
Santiago de Compostela
Brown bear
Cordillera Cantábrica
Potatoes
León
Vigo
Miño
Ourense
Mining
Wh
Embalse de Ricobayo
Wine making
Mining
Vallado
Oporto
Douro
Embalse de Almendra
Potatoes
Salamanca
Fishing
Grapes
Serra da Estrela
Coimbra
Portugal
PORTUGAL
S
Tagus
Embalse de Valde
Embalse de Alcántara
Cáceres
Embalse de Cijara
Santarém
Tagus
Industry
LISBON
Cork trees
Badajoz
Sheep
Setúbal
Alqueva Reservoir
Cabo Espichel
Alentejo
Guadiana
Great M at Co
Sierra Morena
Cordo
Sardines
Iberian lynx
Guadalquivir
Tourism
Citrus fruits
Seville
Flamenco dancers
Algarve
Huelva
Tavira
Dos Hermanas
Lagos
Faro
Golfo de Cádiz
Jerez de la Frontera
Wine making
Barbary ape
Cabo de São Vicente
Fishing
S
Marbe
ATLANTIC OCEAN
Tuna
Cádiz
Costa de la Luz
Gibralta (to U.K
Strait of Gibraltar
Ceuta (to Sp

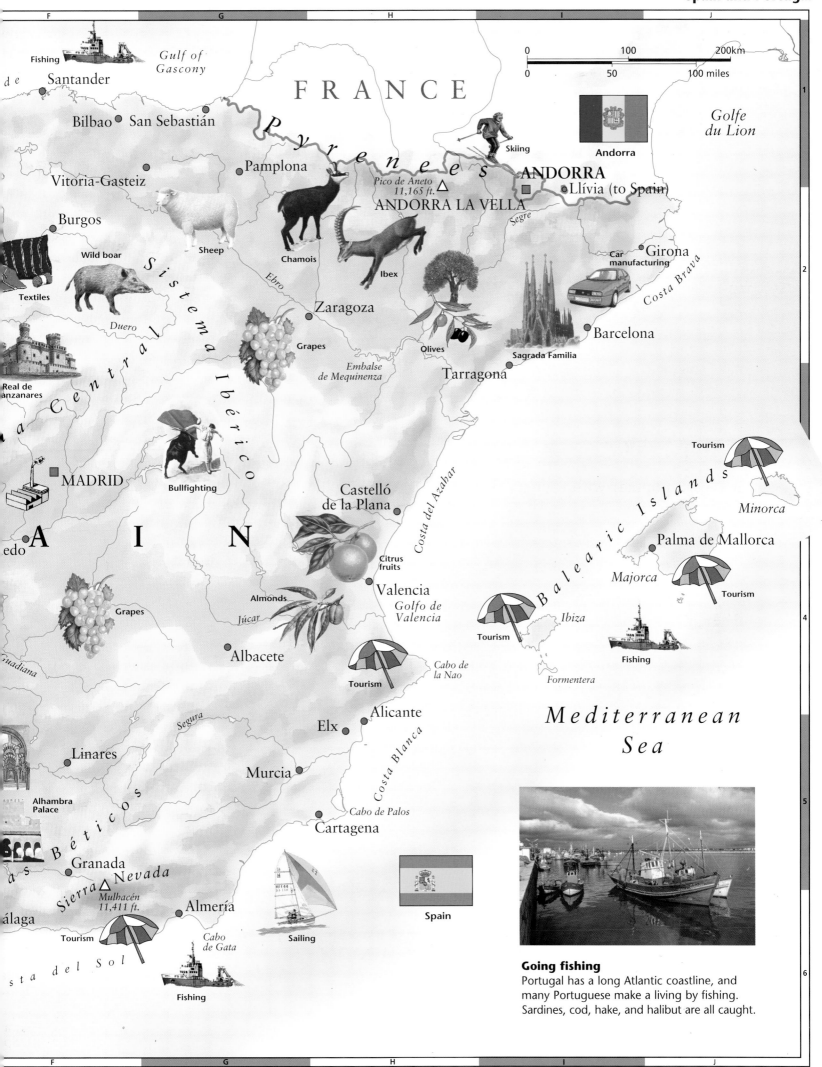

F

Fishing

Gulf of Gascony

Santander

Bilbao ● San Sebastián

FRANCE

Skiing

0   100   200km
0   50   100 miles

Andorra

Golfe du Lion

Vitoria-Gasteiz

Pamplona

P y r e n e e s

Pico de Aneto 11,165 ft. △

ANDORRA

Llívia (to Spain)

Burgos

Sheep

Wild boar

Chamois

ANDORRA LA VELLA

Segre

Car manufacturing

Girona

Textiles

Duero

Ibex

Sistema Ibérico

Zaragoza

Grapes

Olives

Sagrada Familia

Barcelona

Costa Brava

Real de anzanares

Embalse de Mequinenza

Tarragona

Bullfighting

MADRID

Castelló de la Plana

Costa del Azahar

Tourism

Balearic Islands

Minorca

A   I   N

Citrus fruits

Palma de Mallorca

edo

Grapes

Almonds

Júcar

Valencia

Golfo de Valencia

Majorca

Tourism

Ibiza

Tourism

Albacete

Tourism

Cabo de la Nao

Fishing

Segura

Linares

Elx

Alicante

Costa Blanca

Formentera

M e d i t e r r a n e a n S e a

Alhambra Palace

Murcia

Béticos

Cabo de Palos

Granada

Sierra Nevada △

Cartagena

uadiana

Mulhacén 11,411 ft.

Almería

Spain

álaga

Tourism

Cabo de Gata

Sailing

sta del Sol

Fishing

Going fishing

Portugal has a long Atlantic coastline, and many Portuguese make a living by fishing. Sardines, cod, hake, and halibut are all caught.

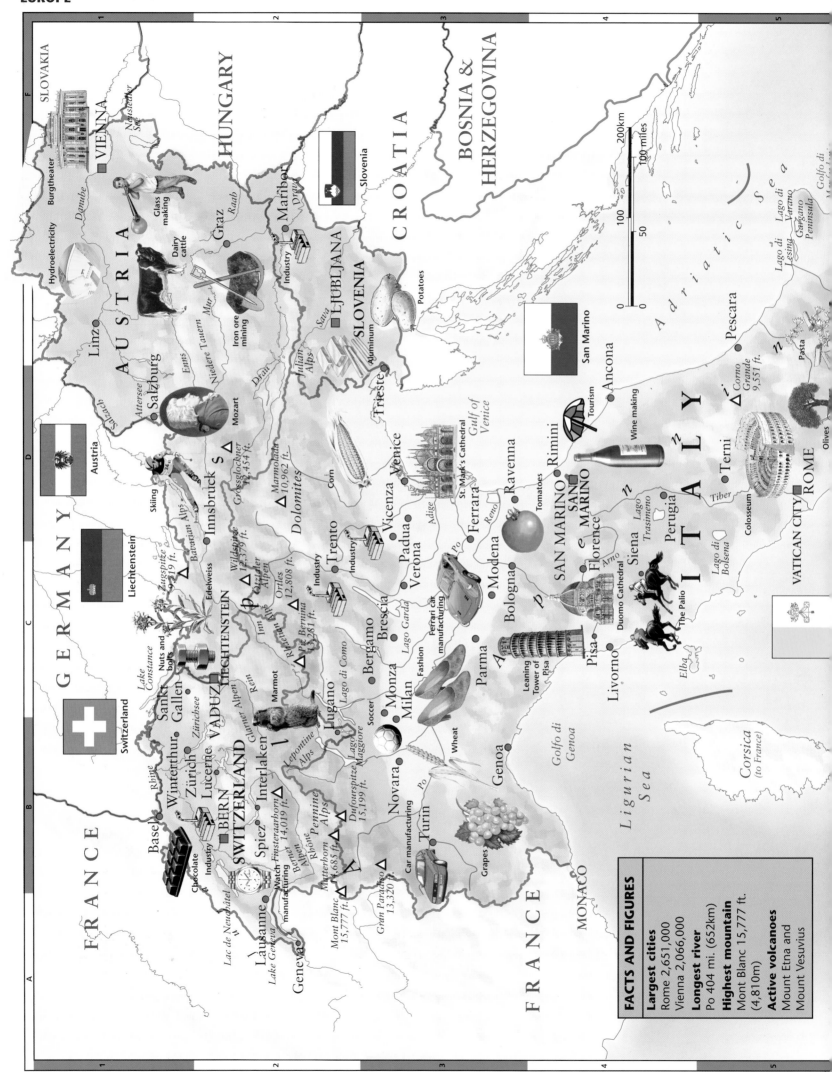

SLOVAKIA

VIENNA

Burgtheater

Neusiedler See

Danube

HUNGARY

Hydroelectricity

Glass making

AUSTRIA

Graz

Raab

Linz

Dairy cattle

Maribor

Drau

Industry

CROATIA

BOSNIA & HERZEGOVINA

Mur

Iron ore mining

Enns

Niedere Tauern

Salzburg

Attersee

Mozart

Drau

Sava

LJUBLJANA

SLOVENIA

Slovenia

Aluminum

Julian Alps

Potatoes

Trieste

Gulf of Venice

200km

100 miles

100

50

Golfo di

Lago di Varano

Gargano Peninsula

Lago di Lesina

A d r i a t i c   S e a

Corno Grande 9,551 ft.

Pescara

San Marino

Ancona

Tourism

Wine making

Rimini

SAN MARINO

SAN MARINO

Ravenna

Ferrara

St. Mark's Cathedral

Venice

Vicenza

Padua

Adige

Verona

Reno

Tomatoes

Po

Modena

Bologna

Terni

Tiber

Perugia

ITALY

Lago Trasimeno

Siena

Florence

Arno

Colosseum

Olives

ROME

VATICAN CITY

Lago di Bolsena

The Palio

Duomo Cathedral

Pisa

Leaning Tower of Pisa

Livorno

Elba

GERMANY

Grossglockner 12,454 ft.

Zugspitze 9,719 ft.

Corn

Marmolada 10,962 ft.

Dolomites

Trento

Wildspitze 12,379 ft.

Ötztaler Alpen

Industry

Industry

Fashion

Ferrari car manufacturing

Lago di Garda

Brescia

Bergamo

Milan

Monza

Soccer

Lago di Como

Novara

Po

Wheat

Parma

Golfo di Genoa

Genoa

A p e n n i n e s

Skiing

Innsbruck

Batarian Alps

Edelweiss

Ortles 12,808 ft.

Rhätian Alps

Pz. Bernina 13,281 ft.

Inn

Liechtenstein

Nuts and bolts

Lake Constance

Zürichsee

VADUZ

LIECHTENSTEIN

Rein

Marmot

Glarner Alpen

Lago Maggiore

Lugano

Lago di Lugano

Lepontine Alps

Austria

Switzerland

Sankt Gallen

Winterthur

Zürich

Lucerne

Interlaken

SWITZERLAND

BERN

Spiez

FRANCE

Basel

Rhine

Chocolate

Industry

Watch manufacturing

Lausanne

Lac de Neuchâtel

Lake Geneva

Geneva

Rhône

Berner Alpen

Finsteraarhorn 14,019 ft.

Dufourspitze 15,199 ft.

Matterhorn 14,685 ft.

Pennine Alps

Mont Blanc 15,777 ft.

Gran Paradiso 13,320 ft.

Car manufacturing

Turin

Po

Grapes

Corsica (to France)

L i g u r i a n   S e a

MONACO

FRANCE

FACTS AND FIGURES

Largest cities
Rome 2,651,000
Vienna 2,066,000

Longest river
Po 404 mi. (652km)

Highest mountain
Mont Blanc 15,777 ft. (4,810m)

Active volcanoes
Mount Etna and Mount Vesuvius

The Alpine States and Italy

The Alpine States—Switzerland, Austria, and Slovenia—take their name from the mountain ranges known as the Alps. These jagged peaks have year-round snow. Winter sports are important there, and in many places cable cars carry tourists and skiers high up into the mountains.

The Alps form the northern border of Italy and overlook the most fertile and densely populated part of the country—the northern plains. Another range of mountains, the Apennines, forms a backbone down the middle of the country. Italy also has a chain of volcanoes, stretching from Mount Vesuvius, close to Naples, to Mount Etna, on the island of Sicily. Both Sicily and Sardinia belong to Italy. Even farther south are the islands that make up Malta.

Two independent countries are found inside Italy. They are San Marino, which lies east of the Apennines, and Vatican City, which is the world's smallest independent nation and lies inside Italy's own capital, Rome.

High mountains
The Dolomites are mountains that lie in the north of Italy and form part of the Alps. Snow covers these peaks all year, and they are home to many glaciers.

Italy

Grapes
Porcupine
Taranto
Golfo di Taranto
Capo Santa Maria di Leuca
Capo Colonne
Olives
Golfo di Squillace
Reggio di Calabria
Capo Spartivento
Messina
Stretto di Messina
Ionian Sea
Appennino Lucano
Mount Vesuvius 4,195 ft.
Citrus fruits
Salerno
Gulf of Salerno
Capri
Ischia
Naples
Stromboli volcano
Stromboli
Isole Eolie
Ustica
Mount Etna 10,988 ft.
Catania
Siracusa
Capo Passero
Olives
Sicily
Oranges
Palermo
Tyrrhenian Sea
Grapes
Marsala
Capo San Vito
Strait of Sicily
Pantelleria
Malta Channel
Gozo
VALLETTA
MALTA
Malta
Malta
Fishing
Linosa
Pelagic Islands
Lampedusa
Ferry
Olives
Mediterranean Sea
Sassari
Tirso
Sardinia
Punta la Marmora 6,016 ft.
Tourism
Grapes
Cagliari
Capo Carbonara
Capo Spartivento
Sant Antioco
Isole Ponziane
Golfo di Gaeta

Eastern and Central Europe

Eastern and central Europe is a region of cold winters and warm summers. In some places, such as in Latvia, winter temperatures drop so low that the seas freeze over. Farther inland bitterly cold winters are common.

During the 1980s and 1990s many of the countries in this area underwent huge political changes. Czechoslovakia split into two separate countries—the Czech Republic and Slovakia. Nations that had previously belonged to the Soviet Union also broke away to become independent countries. These are the Baltic states (Estonia, Latvia, and Lithuania), Belarus, the Ukraine, and Moldova.

Poland shares its borders with seven other countries, but it still has a coastline. Gdansk in the north is a major shipbuilding area. The Czech Republic is a small, hilly, landlocked country in the middle of Europe.

The Ukraine is the second-largest country in Europe. Great quantities of wheat are grown there—it was once known as the "breadbasket of the Soviet Union." Hungary has plains and rolling hills. Estonia is a land of flat plains and lakes and also has more than 800 islands.

FACTS AND FIGURES

Largest cities
Kiev 2,488,000
Warsaw 2,282,000
Budapest 1,812,000
Minsk 1,664,000

Longest river
Danube 1,772 mi. (2,858km)

Highest mountain
Gerlachovsky Stit 8,744 ft. (2,666m)

TALLINN

Pigs

ESTONIA

Tartu

Dairy cattle

Lake Peipus

Lake Pskov

Estonia

Latvia

Lithuania

f ga

RIGA

Potatoes

LATVIA

Beef cattle

Daugavpils

Western Dvina

Churches in Vilnius

ANIA

Chemical industry

unas

VILNIUS

P l a i n

Flax

Vicebsk

Berezina

Machinery

MINSK

Vegetables

Sugar beet

Barley

Eggs

Poultry

BELARUS

Pripet

Pigs

Pripet Marshes

Brest

Wheat farming

Chernobyl

Kiev Reservoir

Industry

KIEV

St. Sophia Cathedral

Dnieper

Dnieper

Desna

Lowlands

Homyel

Common hamster

Steppe polecat

Beautiful city
Prague, the capital of the Czech Republic, has been a bustling city for more than 500 years. It has been a center of culture, learning, and the arts and is also a popular tourist destination.

0   200   400km

0   100   200 miles

Belarus

R U S S I A N

F E D E R A T I O N

Ukraine

L'viv

Oil

o u n t a i n s

Corn

Chernivtsi

Dniester

MOLDOVA

Hungary

Moldova

ROMANIA

Grapes

Prut

Sunflowers

CHISINÂU

V o l y n - P o d o l i a n   U p l a n d

U K R A I N E

Wheat farming

Kremenchuk Reservoir

Cossack dancers

Southern Bug

Kharkov

Steelmaking

Donets

Titanium mining

Industry

Coal mining

Dnipropetrovs'k

Donets'k

Mariupol'

Gulf of Taganrog

Corn

Kakhovka Reservoir

Sunflowers

Black Sea Lowland

Odesa

Gas

Black Sea

Sea of Azov

Kerch

Crimea

Sevastopol'

43

Southeastern Europe

Much of southeastern Europe is mountainous. Farmers graze their sheep and goats on the slopes while growing crops, such as grains and grapes, on the lower land. The climate is changeable—the winters are usually bitterly cold, especially in the north, while the south enjoys milder winters and extremely hot, dry summers. The coastlines along the Adriatic, Black, and Mediterranean seas—and especially the islands in the Aegean Sea—are all popular with tourists. Bosnia & Herzegovina has the shortest coastline in the region—only 12 mi. (20km) on the Adriatic coast.

War has taken its toll on this area. During the 1990s the peoples of Yugoslavia fought bitterly and divided their country into five new countries—Bosnia & Herzegovina, Croatia, Slovenia, Serbia & Montenegro, and Macedonia. Today these countries are beginning to rebuild stable societies.

Greece is a rugged country with many islands. It is also one of the oldest civilizations in Europe. Ancient cultures thrived there, and many fantastic ruins remain to this day.

Gathering roses

Agriculture is very important in southeastern Europe, and many people make their living working on the land. Above, two young women are hard at work harvesting roses on a farm in Bulgaria.

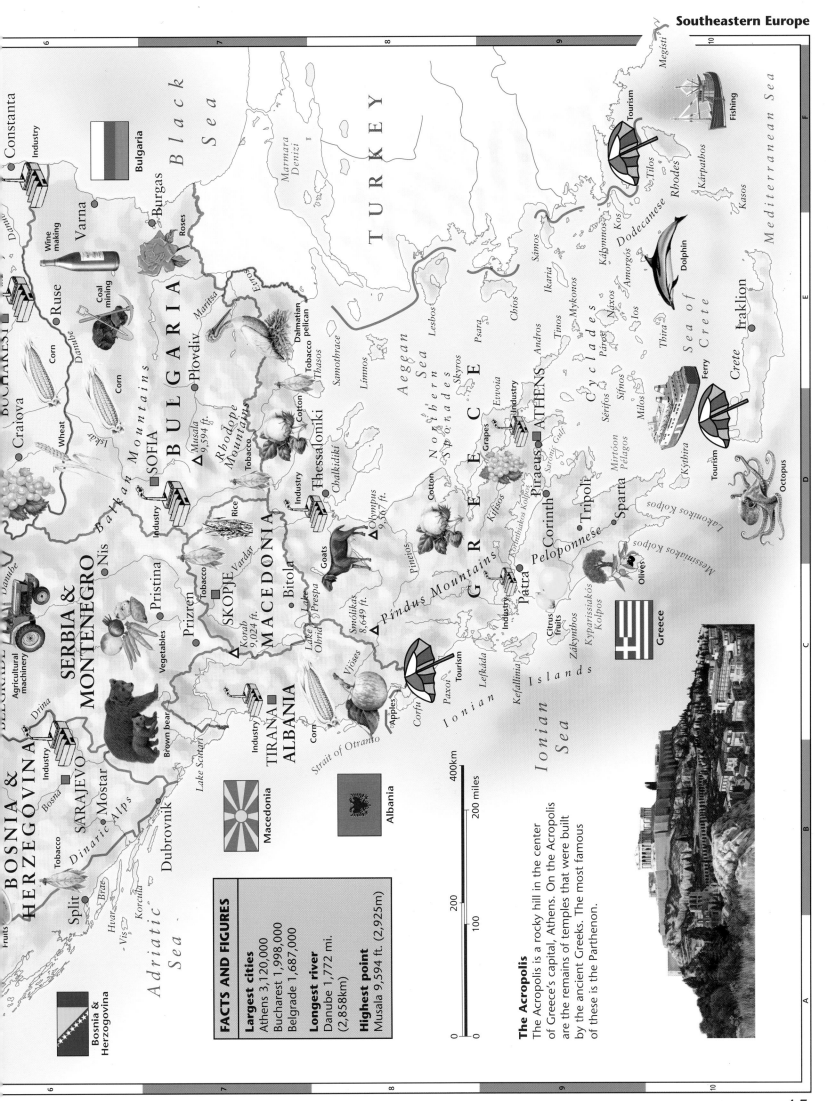

FACTS AND FIGURES

Largest cities
Athens 3,120,000
Bucharest 1,998,000
Belgrade 1,687,000

Longest river
Danube 1,772 mi.
(2,858km)

Highest point
Musala 9,594 ft. (2,925m)

The Acropolis
The Acropolis is a rocky hill in the center of Greece's capital, Athens. On the Acropolis are the remains of temples that were built by the ancient Greeks. The most famous of these is the Parthenon.

Bulgaria
Macedonia
Albania
Greece
Bosnia & Herzegovina

400km
200 miles
200
100
0

45

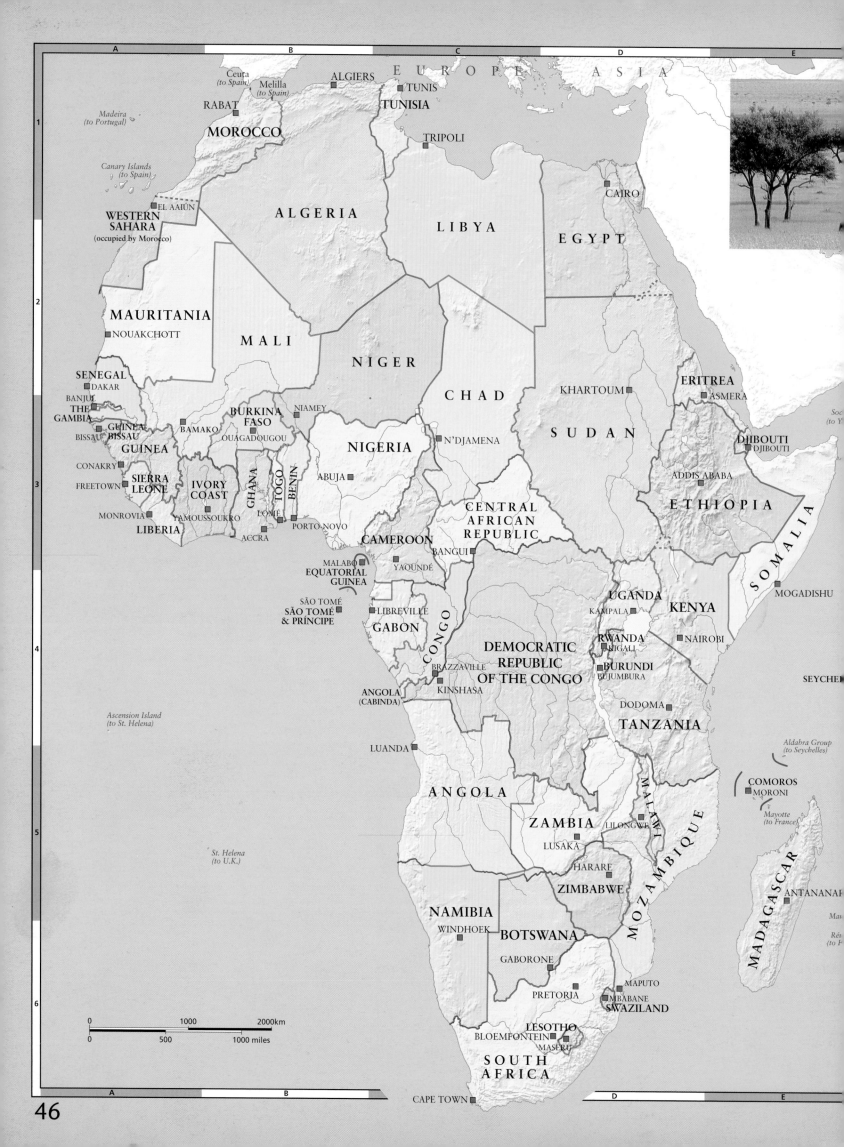

E U R O P E   A S I A

Ceuta
(to Spain)
Melilla
(to Spain)

ALGIERS

TUNIS

TUNISIA

*Madeira
(to Portugal)*

RABAT

MOROCCO

TRIPOLI

CAIRO

*Canary Islands
(to Spain)*

EL AAIÚN

**WESTERN
SAHARA**
(occupied by Morocco)

A L G E R I A

L I B Y A

E G Y P T

*Soc
(to Y*

MAURITANIA

NOUAKCHOTT

M A L I

N I G E R

C H A D

KHARTOUM

ERITREA

ASMERA

SENEGAL

DAKAR

BANJUL

**THE
GAMBIA**

BISSAU

**GUINEA-
BISSAU**

GUINEA

CONAKRY

FREETOWN

**SIERRA
LEONE**

BAMAKO

**BURKINA
FASO**

OUAGADOUGOU

NIAMEY

NIGERIA

ABUJA

N'DJAMENA

S U D A N

DJIBOUTI

DJIBOUTI

ADDIS ABABA

ETHIOPIA

**IVORY
COAST**

YAMOUSSOUKRO

MONROVIA

LIBERIA

GHANA

ACCRA

LOMÉ

TOGO

BENIN

PORTO-NOVO

CAMEROON

BANGUI

**CENTRAL
AFRICAN
REPUBLIC**

S O M A L I A

MOGADISHU

MALABO

**EQUATORIAL
GUINEA**

YAOUNDÉ

SÃO TOMÉ

**SÃO TOMÉ
& PRÍNCIPE**

LIBREVILLE

GABON

CONGO

**DEMOCRATIC
REPUBLIC
OF THE CONGO**

UGANDA

KAMPALA

KENYA

RWANDA

KIGALI

NAIROBI

BURUNDI

BUJUMBURA

*Ascension Island
(to St. Helena)*

BRAZZAVILLE

**ANGOLA
(CABINDA)**

KINSHASA

DODOMA

TANZANIA

SEYCHE

LUANDA

*Aldabra Group
(to Seychelles)*

*St. Helena
(to U.K.)*

A N G O L A

COMOROS

MORONI

*Mayotte
(to France)*

ZAMBIA

LILONGWE

MALAWI

LUSAKA

MOZAMBIQUE

HARARE

MADAGASCAR

ANTANANAR

NAMIBIA

ZIMBABWE

WINDHOEK

Mau

*Ré
(to F*

BOTSWANA

GABORONE

MAPUTO

PRETORIA

MBABANE

SWAZILAND

0   1000   2000km
0   500   1000 miles

LESOTHO

BLOEMFONTEIN

MASERU

**SOUTH
AFRICA**

CAPE TOWN

Going green
During the wet season lush grass grows in the Masai Mara game reserve in Kenya, and the trees burst into life. Animals, including wildebeests, gazelles, giraffes, and lions, come to feast on the fresh foods.

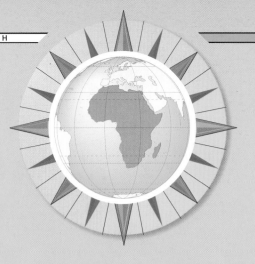

AFRICA

Africa is the second-largest continent, making up around 20 percent of Earth's landmass. It is almost completely surrounded by water. Only a narrow finger of land in Suez in Egypt connects the continent with Asia. When seen from space, Africa looks like it can be divided into three broad bands. The northern band is mostly covered by the Sahara—the largest hot desert in the world. The middle band lies across the equator and is covered with tropical grasslands and rain forests. The grasslands, or savannas, are home to most of Africa's large wildlife, including elephants, rhinoceroses, lions, and leopards. Farther south the lands become drier again. The Great Rift Valley—a crack in Earth's crust—runs through east Africa. Mountains, gorges, and deep lakes, including Lake Victoria, mark this area. The Nile river—the longest river in the world— is found in Africa.

There are more than 50 separate nations in Africa. These are home to many different peoples and cultures.

Lifeblood of Egypt
The Nile river rises in eastern Africa and flows through Egypt, toward the Mediterranean Sea. It has been a major transportation route for more than 5,000 years. Traditional boats, such as this felucca, still travel through its waters today.

Living in Africa
There are many children in Africa, and the population is growing fast. In many places it is difficult to provide enough schools for everyone.

Northern Africa

Much of north Africa consists of dry, arid land, where few people live. The Sahara Desert—one of the hottest places on Earth—stretches more than 3 million sq. mi. (8 million km²) and covers much of the region. The Atlas Mountains surround the desert in the northwest, and the countries there—Algeria, Morocco, and Tunisia—have more rain and fertile land along the Mediterranean coasts. South of the Sahara Desert the land is dry and dusty, with unpredictable rainfalls, and droughts are common. This area is called the Sahel. To the east of the Sahara Desert is the fertile Nile Valley. Most Egyptians live within the Nile Valley, and its capital, Cairo, is one of the busiest cities in the world.

Many of the countries in west Africa are covered with rain forests that support a varied mix of plant and animal life. The region is also relatively rich in natural resources and minerals and is developing industries to process them. Civil wars have taken their toll in recent times, and many countries are still fighting.

Souk shopping
Entertainers and traders make shopping in souks (markets) an exciting event. Here, the Djmaa El Fna square in Marrakech bustles with activity.

48

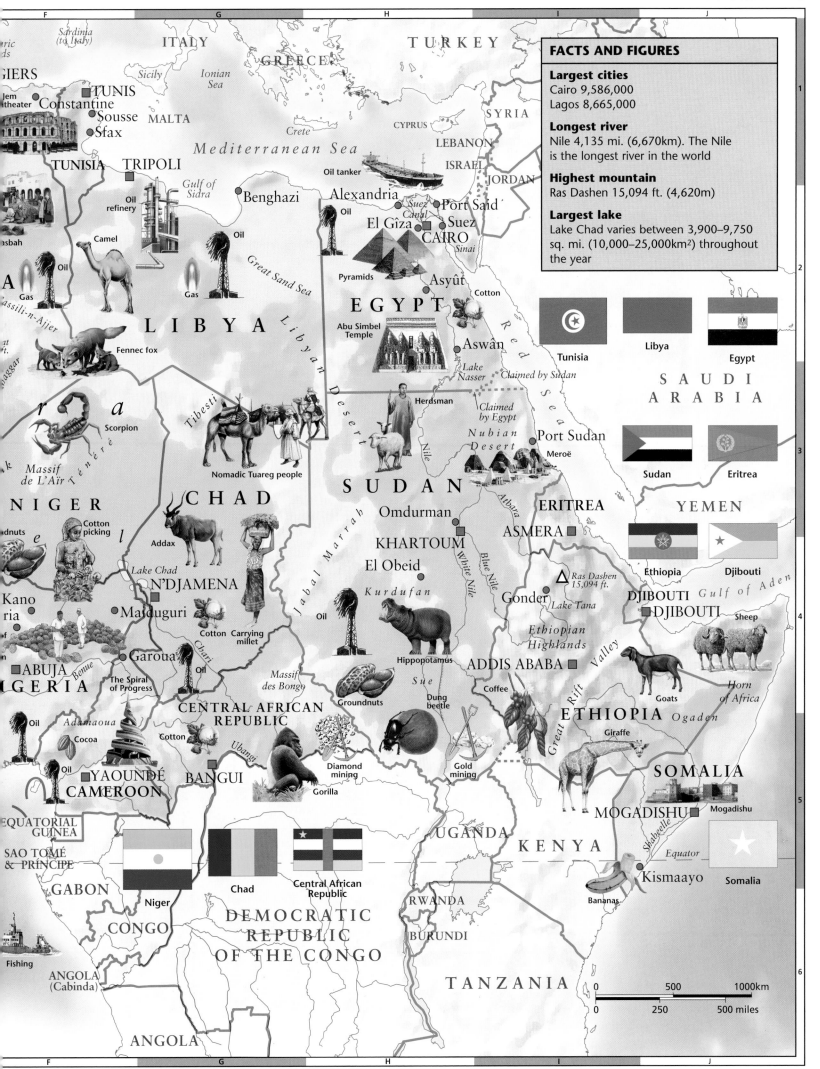

FACTS AND FIGURES

Largest cities
Cairo 9,586,000
Lagos 8,665,000

Longest river
Nile 4,135 mi. (6,670km). The Nile is the longest river in the world

Highest mountain
Ras Dashen 15,094 ft. (4,620m)

Largest lake
Lake Chad varies between 3,900–9,750 sq. mi. (10,000–25,000km²) throughout the year

ITALY

GREECE

TURKEY

Sardinia
(to Italy)

Sicily

MALTA

Ionian
Sea

Crete

CYPRUS

SYRIA

LEBANON

ISRAEL

JORDAN

Mediterranean Sea

GIERS

TUNIS
Constantine
Sousse
Sfax

TUNISIA

TRIPOLI

Oil refinery

Camel

Gas

Oil

Gulf of Sidra

Benghazi

Oil tanker

Alexandria

Oil

Suez Canal

Port Said

El Gîza

Suez

CAIRO

Sinai

LIBYA

Great Sand Sea

Pyramids

EGYPT

Asyût

Cotton

Gas

Libyan Desert

Abu Simbel Temple

Aswân

Red Sea

Lake Nasser

Claimed by Sudan

SAUDI ARABIA

Tunisia

Libya

Egypt

Scorpion

Tibesti

Massif de L'Aïr

Nomadic Tuareg people

Herdsman

Claimed by Egypt

Nubian Desert

Port Sudan

Meroë

Sudan

Eritrea

NIGER

CHAD

Addax

Cotton picking

Lake Chad

N'DJAMENA

Kano

Maiduguri

Cotton

Carrying millet

SUDAN

Jabal Marrah

Omdurman

KHARTOUM

El Obeid

Kurdufan

Nile

White Nile

Blue Nile

Atbara

ERITREA

ASMERA

YEMEN

Ethiopia

Djibouti

Gonder

Ras Dashen 15,094 ft.

Lake Tana

DJIBOUTI

DJIBOUTI

Gulf of Aden

Sheep

ABUJA

Garoua

Benue

The Spiral of Progress

Groundnuts

Chari

Oil

Massif des Bongo

Groundnuts

Hippopotamus

Sue

Coffee

Dung beetle

Gold mining

Ethiopian Highlands

Great Rift Valley

Goats

ADDIS ABABA

ETHIOPIA

Ogaden

Horn of Africa

Giraffe

NIGERIA

Oil

Adamaoua

Cocoa

Cotton

CENTRAL AFRICAN REPUBLIC

Ubangi

Diamond mining

Gorilla

SOMALIA

YAOUNDÉ

CAMEROON

Oil

BANGUI

EQUATORIAL GUINEA

SAO TOMÉ & PRÍNCIPE

GABON

Niger

Chad

Central African Republic

UGANDA

KENYA

MOGADISHU

Mogadishu

Shabeelle

Equator

Somalia

CONGO

DEMOCRATIC REPUBLIC OF THE CONGO

RWANDA

BURUNDI

Kismaayo

Bananas

Fishing

ANGOLA (Cabinda)

ANGOLA

TANZANIA

0   500   1000km
0   250   500 miles

Fennec fox

49

Central and Southern Africa

Lowland covered with lush rain forests stretches across much of the center of Africa, although the rain forests are shrinking as trees are cut down for export. Farther east are huge areas of savannas, with long grasses and scattered trees. Many of Africa's well-known wild animals live around the savannas, and thousands of tourists visit every year to see them.

A volcanic mountain range forms the borders between Rwanda, Uganda, and the Democratic Republic of the Congo. Bitter wars have been fought there in recent years. Farther south lies a high plateau. Many of the rivers there have huge waterfalls such as Victoria Falls on the borders of Zambia and Zimbabwe. These rivers are dammed up for hydroelectricity. Namibia and Botswana are both dry countries with desert areas—the Namib and the Kalahari deserts. South Africa is by far the wealthiest country in Africa, with its rich gold and diamond mines.

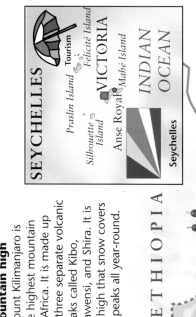

Mountain high

Mount Kilimanjaro is the highest mountain in Africa. It is made up of three separate volcanic peaks called Kibo, Mawensi, and Shira. It is so high that snow covers its peaks all year-round.

SEYCHELLES

Praslin Island
Silhouette Island
Felicité Island
Mahé Island
VICTORIA
Anse Royal
Seychelles

INDIAN OCEAN
Tourism

SOMALIA

Kenya
Rwanda

ETHIOPIA

Lake Turkana
Masai
Great Rift Valley
Mount Kenya 17,052 ft.
Mount Kilimanjaro 19,335 ft.
Mount Kilimanjaro

KENYA

NAIROBI
Leopard
Sisal
Mombasa

Serengeti Plain
Mwanza

SUDAN

Kikuyu bottle
Cotton
Coffee
Kisumu

UGANDA
KAMPALA
Coffee
Uganda

Lake Victoria

KIGALI
RWANDA
BUJUMBURA
BURUNDI

Lake Albert
Lake Edward
Lake Kivu
Bukavu

Aruwimi
Uele
Kisangani
Chimpanzees
Lualaba
Tutsi dancer
Lomani

G r e a t   R i f t

Democratic Republic of the Congo

CENTRAL AFRICAN REPUBLIC

Fishing with traps
Coffee
Congo
Mbandaka

DEMOCRATIC REPUBLIC

C o n g o   B a s i n
Tshuapa
Lukenie
Kasai
Lomami

Ubangi

Ouésso
CONGO
Congo
Coffee
BRAZZAVILLE

Congo
Coffee

Mbuti Pygmy

GABON
Cocoa
Port-Gentil
Oil rig

CAMEROON

São Tomé & Príncipe
MALABO
Bata
LIBREVILLE

EQUATORIAL GUINEA
Bioko
Equatorial Guinea

Príncipe
SÃO TOMÉ & PRÍNCIPE
São Tomé
SÃO TOMÉ

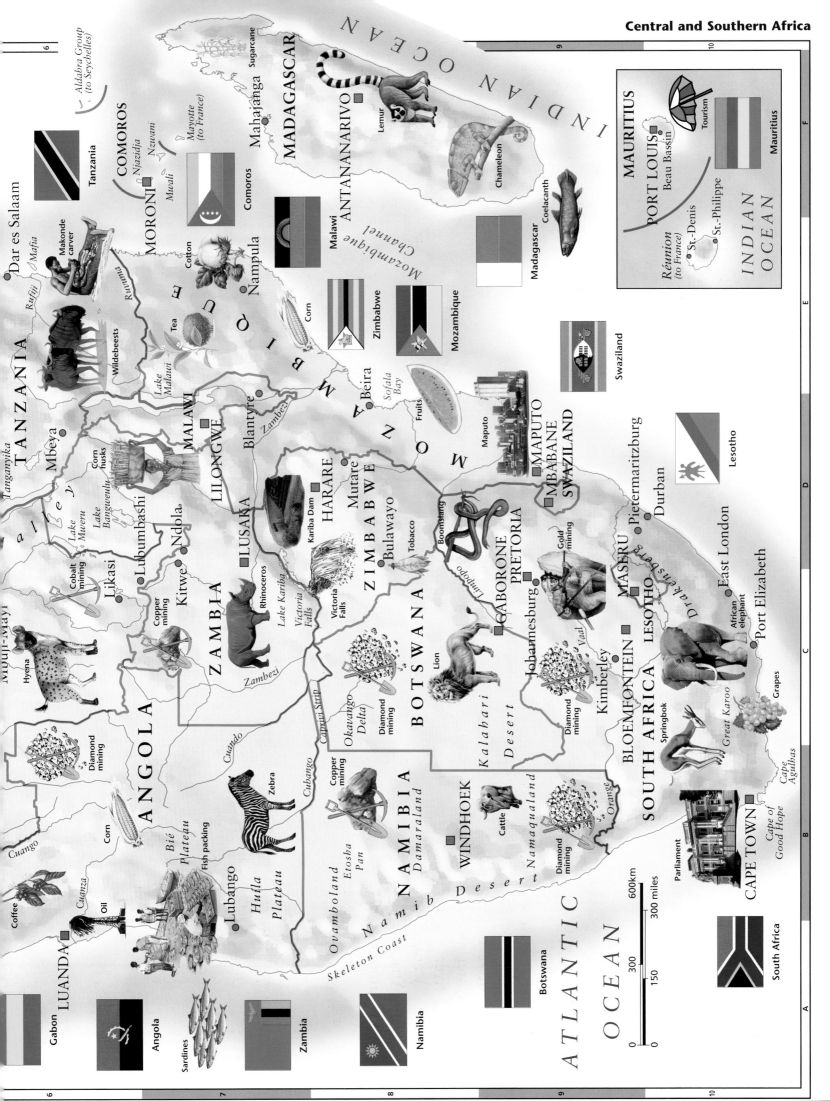

INDIAN OCEAN

Aldabra Group
(to Seychelles)

Sugarcane

MADAGASCAR

Mahajanga

Lemur

ANTANANARIVO

Chameleon

Coelacanth

COMOROS

Nzwani

Niazidja

Tanzania

Mwali

MORONI

Comoros

Mayotte
(to France)

Dar es Salaam

Makonde
carver

Mafia

Rufiji

Ruvuma

Cotton

Nampula

Malawi

ANTANANARIVO

Mozambique Channel

MAURITIUS

PORT LOUIS
Beau Bassin

Tourism

Réunion
(to France)

St.-Denis

St.-Philippe

Mauritius

INDIAN
OCEAN

Madagascar

Coelacanth

TANZANIA

Wildebeests

Tea

Corn

Zimbabwe

Mozambique

Mbeya

Lake Malawi

MALAWI

LILONGWE

Blantyre

Zambezi

Beira

Sofala
Bay

Fruits

Maputo

Swaziland

MAPUTO

MBABANE

SWAZILAND

Pietermaritzburg

Durban

Lesotho

Tanganyika

Lake Mweru

Lake Bangweulu

Lubumbashi

Ndola

HARARE

Kariba Dam

Mutare

Boomslang

PRETORIA

Gold
mining

Maseru

East London

Lubumbashi

Cobalt
mining

Likasi

Kitwe

Copper
mining

LUSAKA

Rhinoceros

Lake Kariba

Victoria
Falls

ZIMBABWE

Bulawayo

Tobacco

GABORONE

Johannesburg

Vaal

Kimberley

MASERU

LESOTHO

African
elephant

Port Elizabeth

Muburu-Mayi

Hyena

ZAMBIA

Zambezi

Victoria
Falls

Lion

Diamond
mining

BOTSWANA

Kalahari Desert

Diamond
mining

BLOEMFONTEIN

Springbok

SOUTH AFRICA

Great Karoo

Grapes

Drakensberg

ANGOLA

Diamond
mining

Cuando

Cubango

Copper
mining

Okavango
Delta

Diamond
mining

Zebra

Caprivi Strip

Orange

Cape
Agulhas

Coffee

Cuango

Corn

Bié
Plateau

Lubango

Huíla
Plateau

Etosha
Pan

NAMIBIA

Damaraland

WINDHOEK

Cattle

Namaqualand

Diamond
mining

Oil

LUANDA

Cuanza

Fish packing

Ovamboland

Namib Desert

Skeleton Coast

Gabon

Sardines

Angola

Zambia

Namibia

Botswana

600km

300 miles

300

150

ATLANTIC
OCEAN

Parliament

CAPE TOWN

Cape of
Good Hope

South Africa

Severnaya Zemlya

New Siberian Isla

R U S S I A N   F E D E R A T I O N

E U R O P E

Sakl

ASTANA

K A Z A K H S T A N

ULAN BATOR

M O N G O L I A

Hokka

GEORGIA
TBILISI
ARMENIA
YEREVAN
BAKU
AZERBAIJAN
ANKARA
TURKEY

BISHKEK

UZBEKISTAN

KYRGYZSTAN

TASHKENT

TURKMENISTAN

TAJIKISTAN

DUSHANBE

ASHGABAT

BEIJING

NORTH
KOREA
PYONGYANG

JAP

CYPRUS
NICOSIA
SYRIA
LEBANON
DAMASCUS
BEIRUT
BAGHDAD
JERUSALEM
AMMAN
ISRAEL
JORDAN
IRAQ

TEHRAN

I R A N

KABUL

AFGHANISTAN

ISLAMABAD

C H I N A

SEOUL
SOUTH
KOREA

Honshu

TO

KUWAIT
KUWAIT

MANAMA
BAHRAIN
RIYADH
DOHA
QATAR
ABU DHABI
UNITED
ARAB
EMIRATES
MUSCAT

OMAN

P A K I S T A N

NEW DELHI

NEPAL
KATHMANDU
BHUTAN
THIMPHU

BANGLADESH
DHAKA

T'AIPEI
TAIWAN

*Ryukyu
Islands*

S A U D I
A R A B I A

OMAN

MYANMAR
(BURMA)

LAOS

HANOI

Hainan

SANA
YEMEN

*Socotra
(to Yemen)*

*Laccadive Islands
(to India)*

I N D I A

*Andaman
Islands
(to India)*

RANGOON

VIENTIANE

THAILAND

VIETNAM

Luzon

MANILA

A F R I C A

BANGKOK

PHNOM
PENH

CAMBODIA

PHILIPPINES

Mindanao

COLOMBO
SRI JAYEWARDENEPURA
SRI
LANKA

*Nicobar
Islands
(to India)*

MALE
MALDIVES

BRUNEI
BANDAR SERI BEGAWAN

M A L A Y S I A

KUALA
LUMPUR
SINGAPORE
SINGAPORE

Borneo

Sulawesi

Moluccas

IRIAN
JAYA

*British
Indian Ocean
Territory
(to U.K.)*

JAKARTA

I N D O N E S I A

Sumatra

Java

DILI
EAST TIMOR

A U S T R A L A S

0   1000   2000km
0   500   1000 miles

Wrangel Island

ASIA

Asia is the largest continent. It makes up around 35 percent of Earth's land surface and is home to 60 percent of the population. It stretches from Turkey and the Ural Mountains in Russia in the west to the Pacific Ocean in the east and from the icy Arctic Ocean in the north to the tropical islands of Indonesia, with their steamy rain forests, in the south. The landscape of this vast area is varied. The world's highest mountain, Mount Everest in the Himalayas, is always covered with snow, while elsewhere, in the middle of the continent, there are huge expanses of bare, rocky deserts. Frozen plains cover much of the far north. Lake Baikal—the world's deepest lake— is in Asia, along with some of the world's greatest rivers—the Chang Jiang (Yangtze) and the Ganges.

Asia contains three huge and populous countries—the Russian Federation, China, and India— as well as several that are not as large. It is a diverse continent with a wide variety of peoples, beliefs, languages, and lifestyles. It contains some of the world's poorest regions and wealthiest big cities.

On top of the world
The Himalayas are the highest mountain range in the world. The mountains stretch for 1,488 mi. (2,400km), and snow and glaciers cover many of the peaks all year-round.

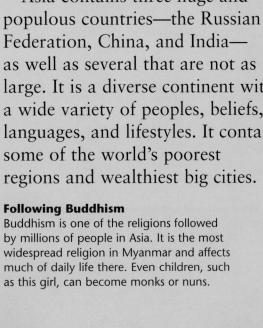

Following Buddhism
Buddhism is one of the religions followed by millions of people in Asia. It is the most widespread religion in Myanmar and affects much of daily life there. Even children, such as this girl, can become monks or nuns.

The Russian Federation

The Russian Federation is the largest country in the world. It stretches across both Europe and Asia. Most of the people live to the west of the Ural Mountains in the European part of the country. Large birch and conifer forests cover the region, and the Volga river provides water.

The eastern part of the Russian Federation is in Asia. This vast area includes regions of marshland and the largest coniferous forest in the world, as well as grassy plains known as steppes. Most of Russia's grain is grown on large farms there.

The Russian Federation was formed in 1991 after the earlier breakup of the communist Soviet Union. Many former states became independent countries. Under Soviet rule industries were run by the state, and many were outdated. Today the country is modernizing many of its industries and farming techniques.

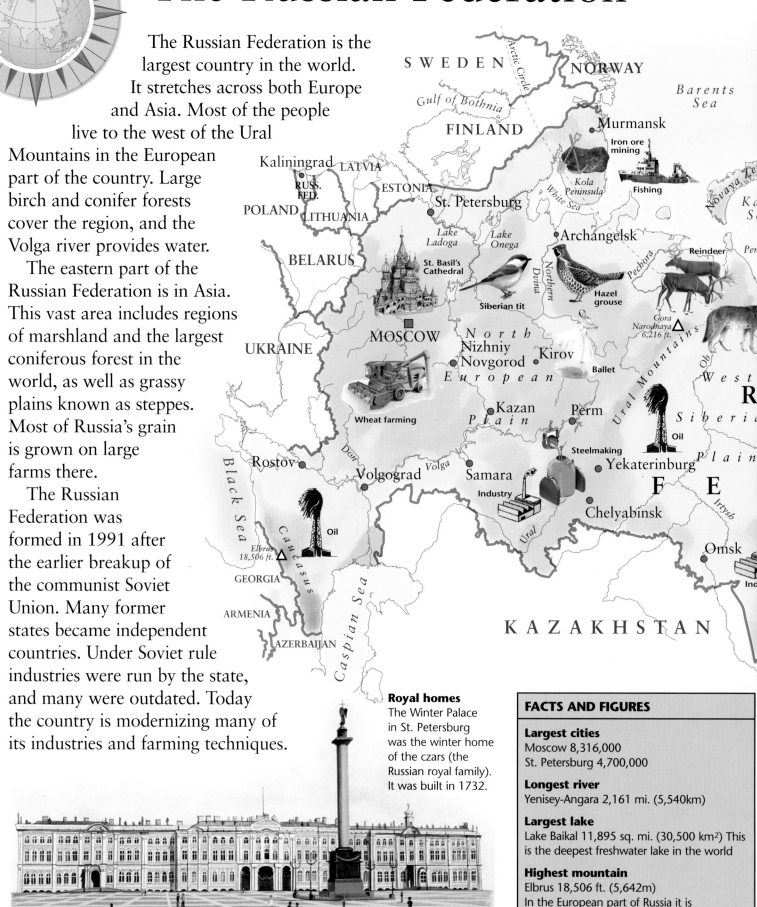

Royal homes
The Winter Palace in St. Petersburg was the winter home of the czars (the Russian royal family). It was built in 1732.

FACTS AND FIGURES

Largest cities
Moscow 8,316,000
St. Petersburg 4,700,000

Longest river
Yenisey-Angara 2,161 mi. (5,540km)

Largest lake
Lake Baikal 11,895 sq. mi. (30,500 km²) This is the deepest freshwater lake in the world

Highest mountain
Elbrus 18,506 ft. (5,642m)
In the European part of Russia it is the highest point in Europe

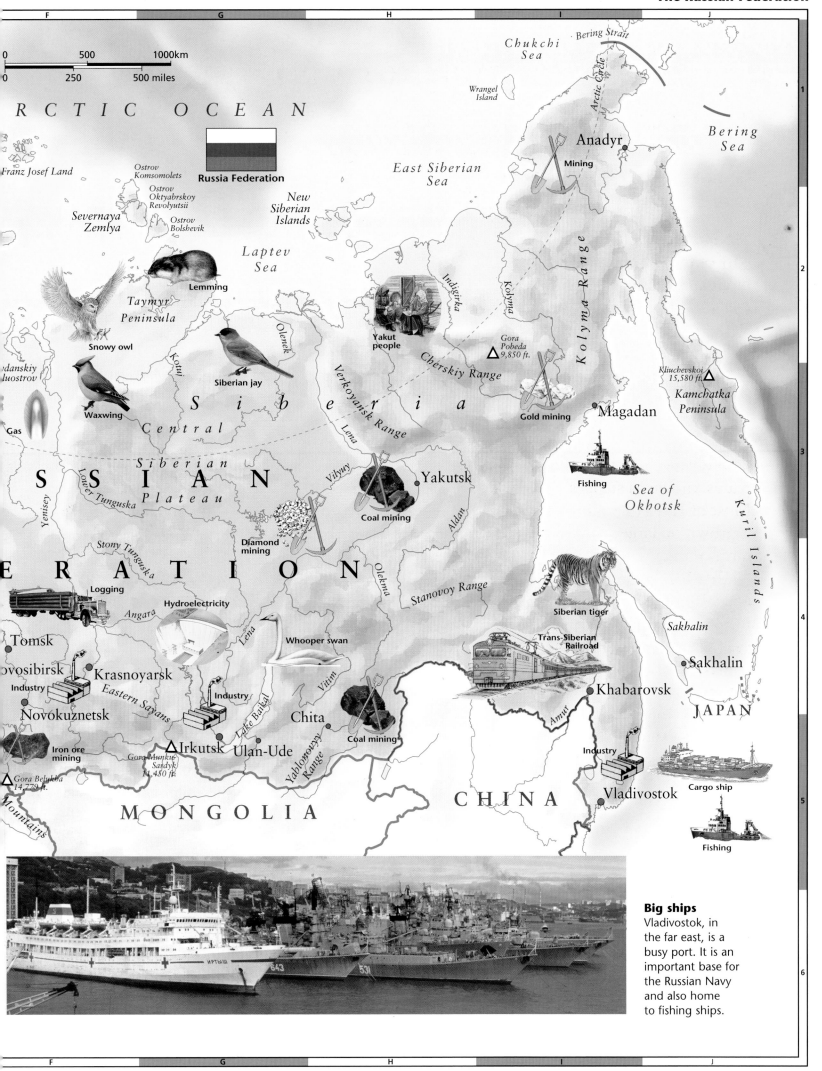

0   500   1000km

0   250   500 miles

A R C T I C   O C E A N

Franz Josef Land

Ostrov Komsomolets

Ostrov Oktyabrskoy Revolyutsii

Ostrov Bolshevik

Severnaya Zemlya

Laptev Sea

New Siberian Islands

East Siberian Sea

Chukchi Sea

Bering Strait

Wrangel Island

Anadyr

Mining

Bering Sea

Russia Federation

Lemming

Taymyr Peninsula

Snowy owl

danskiy luostrov

Siberian jay

Waxwing

Kottii

Olenek

S i b e r i a

Central

Verkoyansk Range

Indigirka

Kolyma

Yakut people

Chérskiy Range

Gora Pobeda 9,850 ft.

Kolyma Range

Kliuchevskoi 15,580 ft.

Kamchatka Peninsula

Gas

S i b e r i a n

Plateau

Lena

Vilyuy

Gold mining

Magadan

Yenisey

Lower Tunguska

Diamond mining

Coal mining

Yakutsk

Aldan

Fishing

Sea of Okhotsk

Stony Tunguska

Kuril Islands

Logging

Angara

Hydroelectricity

Lena

Whooper swan

Olekma

Stanovoy Range

Siberian tiger

Tomsk

ovosibirsk

Industry

Krasnoyarsk

Eastern Sayans

Industry

Lake Baikal

Vitim

Trans-Siberian Railroad

Sakhalin

Sakhalin

Novokuznetsk

Chita

Yablonovyy Range

Khabarovsk

Iron ore mining

Irkutsk

Gora Munku-Sardyk 11,450 ft.

Ulan-Ude

Coal mining

Amur

J A P A N

Gora Belukha 14,779 ft.

Industry

Vladivostok

Cargo ship

Mountains

M O N G O L I A

C H I N A

Fishing

Big ships
Vladivostok, in the far east, is a busy port. It is an important base for the Russian Navy and also home to fishing ships.

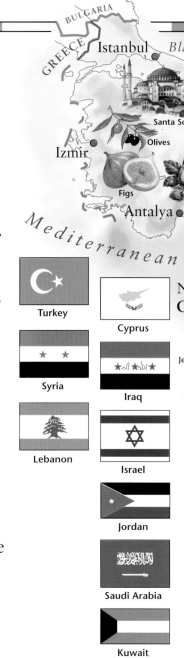

West Asia

Three continents—Europe, Asia, and Africa—all meet in west Asia, which is also known as the Middle East. It is the only place on Earth where this happens, and the region has been used for a long time by traders. The world's first cities grew up in the area between the Tigris and Euphrates rivers around 5,500 years ago.

West Asia's northern borders are made up of mountains and seas. To the west is the Mediterranean Sea, while farther south are the warm waters of the Red Sea, The Gulf, and the Indian Ocean. The Tigris and Euphrates rivers bring fertility to the lands that surround them, but most of west Asia is desert or semidesert with a climate that is mostly hot and dry. Saudi Arabia's "Empty Quarter" is one of the most inhospitable places on Earth.

Three of the world's most widespread religions—Judaism, Christianity and Islam—have their roots in west Asia. Oil and natural gas have brought great wealth to many countries, and the region produces more than one third of the world's daily oil output. Unfortunately, both oil and religion have led to bitter conflicts. There are border disputes within Israel, which was founded in 1948 from an area called Palestine, and there has been conflict ever since. Thousands of Palestinians have been displaced and want to set up their own country in their ancient homelands. Fighting continues in many parts of the region and the area is politically unsettled.

Turkey

Cyprus

Syria

Iraq

Lebanon

Israel

Jordan

Saudi Arabia

Kuwait

FACTS AND FIGURES

Largest cities
Istanbul 8,953,000
Tehran 7,038,000
Baghdad 4,958,000

Longest river
Euphrates 1,674 mi. (2,700km)

Highest mountain
Qolleh-ye Damavand 18,381 ft. (5,618m)

Oldest city
Damascus, the capital of Syria, is the world's oldest continuously inhabited city. It is around 4,500 years old

A place to worship
Istanbul is one of Turkey's most attractive cities. Islam is the national religion, and the city has many beautiful mosques, such as the Suleymaniye Mosque, shown.

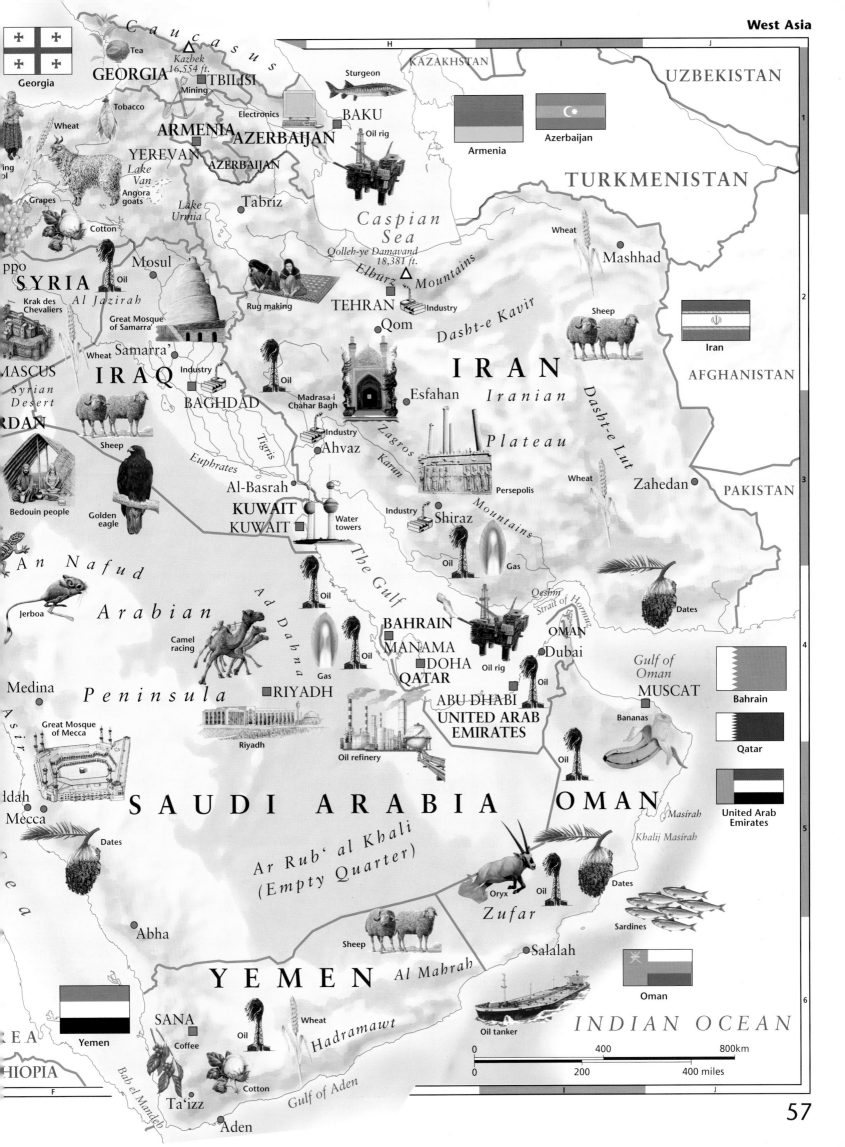

Georgia

GEORGIA
Caucasus
Kazbek 16,554 ft.
Tea
Tobacco
Wheat
Grapes
Cotton
Angora goats
TBILISI
Mining
Electronics
ARMENIA
AZERBAIJAN
YEREVAN
Lake Van
Lake Urmia
AZERBAIJAN
Tabriz
Sturgeon
BAKU
Oil rig

KAZAKHSTAN

UZBEKISTAN

Armenia
Azerbaijan

TURKMENISTAN

Caspian Sea
Qolleh-ye Damavand 18,381 ft.
Elburz Mountains
Wheat
Mashhad

Iran

AFGHANISTAN

SYRIA
Oil
Al Jazirah
Krak des Chevaliers
Great Mosque of Samarra'
Rug making
TEHRAN
Industry
Qom
Sheep
IRAN
Dasht-e Kavir
Dasht-e Lut

Wheat
Samarra'
IRAQ
Industry
BAGHDAD
Oil
Madrasa-i Chahar Bagh
Industry
Esfahan
Iranian Plateau

DAMASCUS
Syrian Desert
RDAN
Sheep
Bedouin people
Golden eagle
Tigris
Euphrates
Ahvaz
Al-Basrah
Karun
Zagros Mountains
Persepolis
Industry
Shiraz
Wheat
Zahedan

PAKISTAN

An Nafud
Jerboa
Arabian
KUWAIT
KUWAIT
Water towers
Oil
Oil
Gas
Mountains

Ad Dahna
Camel racing
Oil
Gas
BAHRAIN
MANAMA
DOHA
QATAR
Oil rig
Qeshm
Strait of Hormuz
OMAN
Dubai
Oil
Gulf of Oman
MUSCAT
Dates
Bananas

Medina
Peninsula
RIYADH
Great Mosque of Mecca
Riyadh
Oil refinery
ABU DHABI
UNITED ARAB EMIRATES
Oil

Bahrain
Qatar
United Arab Emirates

ldah
Mecca

SAUDI ARABIA

OMAN
Masirah
Khalij Masirah

Dates
Ar Rub' al Khali (Empty Quarter)
Oryx
Oil
Zufar
Dates
Sardines

Abha
Sheep
Salalah

YEMEN
Al Mahrah
Oil tanker

Oman

E A
SANA
Coffee
Wheat
Hadramawt
Cotton
Bab el Mandeb
Ta'izz
Gulf of Aden
Aden

HIOPIA

Yemen

INDIAN OCEAN

| 0 | 400 | 800km |
| 0 | 200 | 400 miles |

Central Asia

Much of Central Asia is mountainous, with fertile plains and rocky deserts. The world's second-highest mountain, K2, is found there in the Karakoram mountain range in Pakistan. Highlands make up much of Afghanistan and have an effect on the climate. Northerly winds bring cold winters, but summers are hot and dry. Many of the countries in central Asia are landlocked (surrounded by other countries, with no coasts), and because they are so far from the sea, their climates tend to be dry without much rainfall. Kazakhstan has cold, snowy winters and warm summers.

There are many freshwater lakes in the region, and water from these is used to irrigate crops. However, this can cause problems—so much water has been taken from the Amu and Syr rivers in Uzbekistan that the Aral Sea is drying out. The mighty Indus river flows through Pakistan. Its waters support life along the fertile plains. In southwestern Pakistan there are large areas of deserts. Throughout history the lands of Pakistan have been invaded and controlled by many different nations. Peaceful settlers have also made their homes there, and the population reflects this racial mix.

Traditional lifestyles
Millions of Afghans live a nomadic way of life, tending small flocks of goats and sheep. They live in felt-lined tents called yurts, which can be packed up and moved around easily.

RUSSIAN FEDERATION

Altay Mountains

Lake Zaysan

Irtysh

Coal mining

Gold mining

Pavlodar

Wheat

ASTANA

Qaraghandy

Industry

KAZAKHSTAN

Kazakh Uplands

Folk dancers

Lake Tengiz

Ishim

Kirgiz Steppe

Tobo

Great bustard

Mining

Myrzobay

Wheat

Kazakhstan

Oral

Ural

Caspian Depression

Atyrau

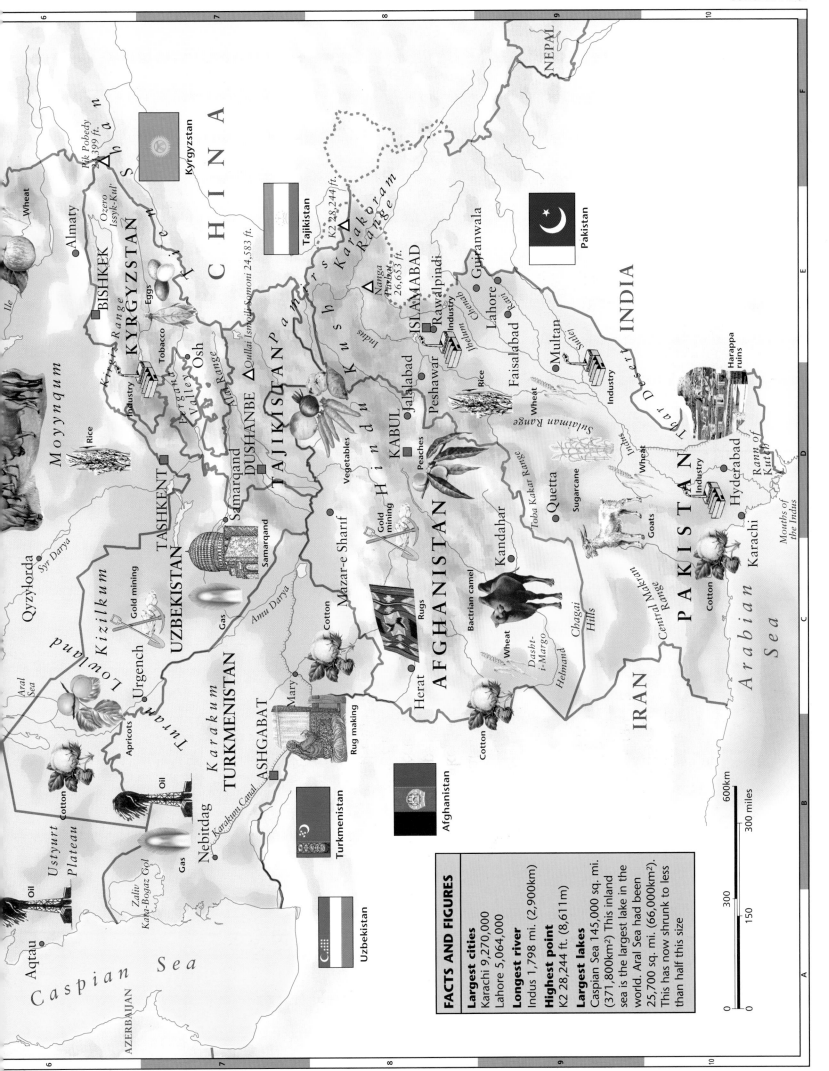

6

7

8

9

10

F

E

D

C

B

A

NEPAL

Kyrgyzstan

Tajikistan

Pakistan

C H I N A

Pik Pobedy
24,399 ft.

Wheat

Ile

Almaty

Ozero Issyk-Kul'

T i e n   S h a n

Kirgiz Range

BISHKEK

KYRGYZSTAN

Eggs

Tobacco

Osh

Industry

Fergana Valley

Alay Range

Rice

K2 28,244 ft.

K a r a k o r a m   R a n g e

Nanga Parbat
26,653 ft.

Gujranwala

ISLAMABAD

Rawalpindi

Industry

Jhelum

Chenab

Lahore

Ravi

Faisalabad

INDIA

Multan

Sutlej

Industry

Harappa
ruins

Indus

T h a r   D e s e r t

P a m i r s

H i n d u   K u s h

Peshawar

Jalalabad

Rice

Wheat

Sulaiman Range

Indus

Wheat

Qullai Ismoili Somoni 24,583 ft.

DUSHANBE

Samarqand

TAJIKISTAN

Vegetables

KABUL

Peaches

Gold mining

Mazar-e Sharif

Samarqand

Amu Darya

TASHKENT

UZBEKISTAN

Gold mining

K i z i l k u m

Rice

Moyynqum

Qyzylorda

Syr Darya

AFGHANISTAN

Rugs

Cotton

Bactrian camel

Wheat

Quetta

Toba Kakar Range

Sugarcane

Goats

Central Makran Range

PAKISTAN

Industry

Hyderabad

Ramm of Kutch

Mouths of the Indus

Cotton

Karachi

A r a b i a n   S e a

Dasht-i-Margo

Kandahar

Helmand

Chagai Hills

IRAN

Herat

Cotton

Gas

K a r a k u m

TURKMENISTAN

Turan Lowland

Urgench

Apricots

Aral Sea

Ustyurt Plateau

Oil

Cotton

Oil

Gas

Nebitdag

ASHGABAT

Mary

Rug making

Karakum Canal

Zaliv Kara-Bogaz Gol

Aqtau

C a s p i a n   S e a

AZERBAIJAN

Turkmenistan

Afghanistan

Uzbekistan

600km

300 miles

300

150

0

0

FACTS AND FIGURES

Largest cities
Karachi 9,270,000
Lahore 5,064,000

Longest river
Indus 1,798 mi. (2,900km)

Highest point
K2 28,244 ft. (8,611m)

Largest lakes
Caspian Sea 145,000 sq. mi. (371,800km²) This inland sea is the largest lake in the world. Aral Sea had been 25,700 sq. mi. (66,000km²). This has now shrunk to less than half this size

59

South Asia

South Asia is bordered by the Thar Desert in the northwest and the Himalayas, a great chain of towering mountains, in the north and east. The Himalayas contain some of the highest mountains in the world, including the highest of all, Mount Everest. They are so high that they are covered with snow all year-round, and most of the people in Bhutan and Nepal live in the more sheltered valleys in the south.

In Bangladesh, by contrast, most of the land is low-lying and flat. The mighty Ganges and Brahmaputra rivers flow through fertile valleys into the sea. Every year monsoon rains swell these rivers and can cause terrible floods.

Much of India is covered with rolling plateau land, where farmers grow corn and millet and graze their animals. More than 60 percent of the country's large population makes its living from agriculture, but the country is also home to large-scale industries and huge, crowded cities.

Sri Lanka is a mountainous island off the southern coast of India. It is fringed with beautiful beaches. A fertile plain, which is an important tea growing area, is found inland.

Religious river
The Ganges is a sacred river to followers of the Hindu religion. They make pilgrimages to the river to bathe in its cleansing waters. Steps, or ghats, have been built along its banks to help people get in and out of the water.

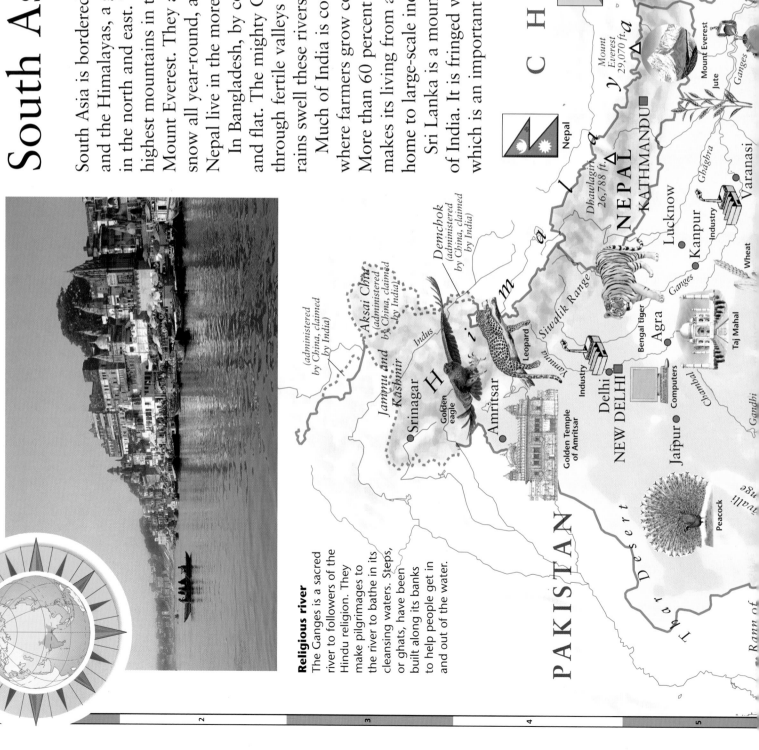

CHINA

Kula Kangri
24,777 ft.

THIMPHU BHUTAN
Bhutan

Asian elephant
Brahmaputra
Asian rhinoceros
Naga Hills

BANGLADESH

Mount Everest
29,070 ft.

Dhaulagiri
26,788 ft.

NEPAL
KATHMANDU
Nepal

Mount Everest
Jute
Ganges

Aksai Chin
(administered by China, claimed by India)

Demchok
(administered by China, claimed by India)

Jammu and Kashmir
(administered by China, claimed by India)

Srinagar
Golden eagle

Amritsar
Golden Temple of Amritsar

Ghaghra
Lucknow
Kanpur
Industry
Wheat

Siwalik Range
Ganges
Bengal tiger
Leopard
Yamuna
Agra
Taj Mahal

Himalaya

Thar Desert

PAKISTAN

Industry
Delhi
NEW DELHI
Computers
Jaipur
Chambal
Peacock
Gandhi
Aravalli Range

Indus

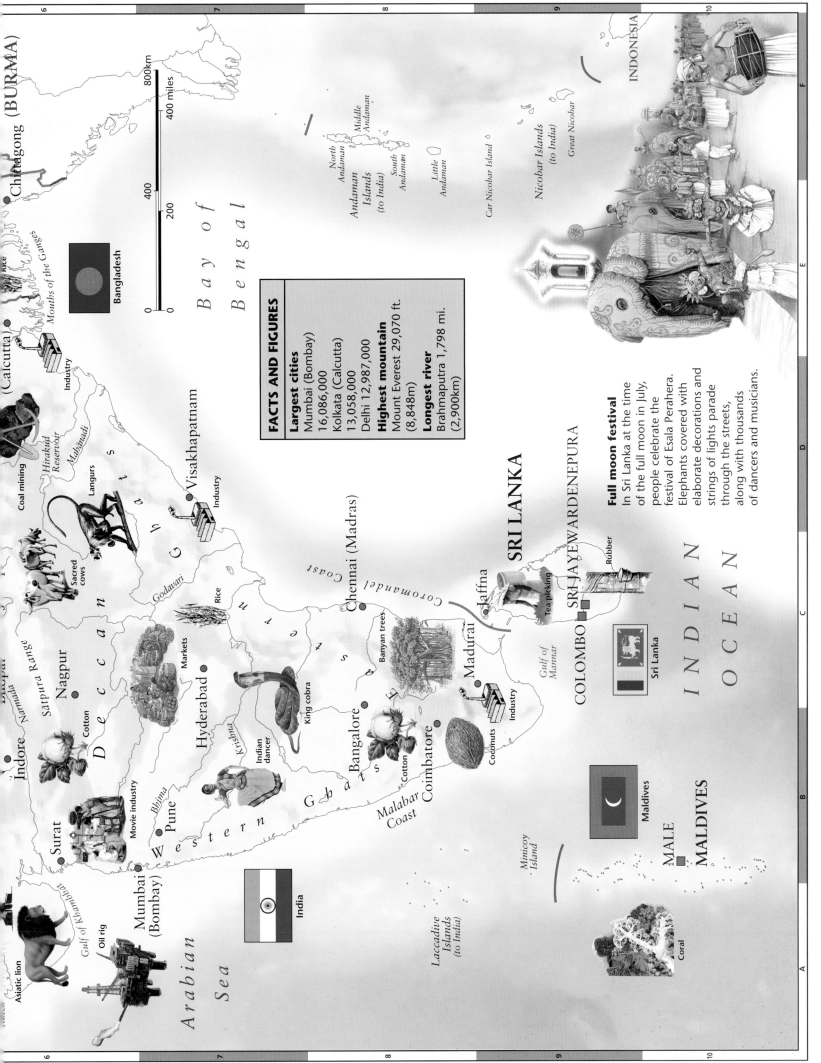

Chittagong (BURMA)

Calcutta

Mouths of the Ganges

Bangladesh

800km
400 miles
400
200
0

Bay of Bengal

North Andaman
Middle Andaman
South Andaman
Andaman Islands (to India)
Little Andaman
Car Nicobar Island
Nicobar Islands (to India)
Great Nicobar

INDONESIA

FACTS AND FIGURES

Largest cities
Mumbai (Bombay) 16,086,000
Kolkata (Calcutta) 13,058,000
Delhi 12,987,000

Highest mountain
Mount Everest 29,070 ft. (8,848m)

Longest river
Brahmaputra 1,798 mi. (2,900km)

Full moon festival
In Sri Lanka at the time of the full moon in July, people celebrate the festival of Esala Perahera. Elephants covered with elaborate decorations and strings of lights parade through the streets, along with thousands of dancers and musicians.

Industry

Coal mining
Hirakud Reservoir
Mahanadi
Langurs
Visakhapatnam
Industry
Sacred cows
Deccan
Godavari
Rice
Ghats
Nagpur
Cotton
Markets
Hyderabad
Krishna
Indian dancer
King cobra
Indore
Sātpura Range
Namada
Surat
Gulf of Khambhat
Oil rig
Mumbai (Bombay)
Movie industry
Bhima
Pune
Western Ghats
Arabian Sea
India
Bangalore
Cotton
Coimbatore
Coconuts
Banyan trees
Chennai (Madras)
Coromandel Coast
Madurai
Jaffna
SRI LANKA
SRI JAYEWARDENEPURA
Tea picking
Rubber
COLOMBO
Gulf of Mannar
Sri Lanka
Malabar Coast
Industry
INDIAN OCEAN
Minicoy Island
Laccadive Islands (to India)
MALDIVES
MALE
Maldives
Coral
Asiatic lion

61

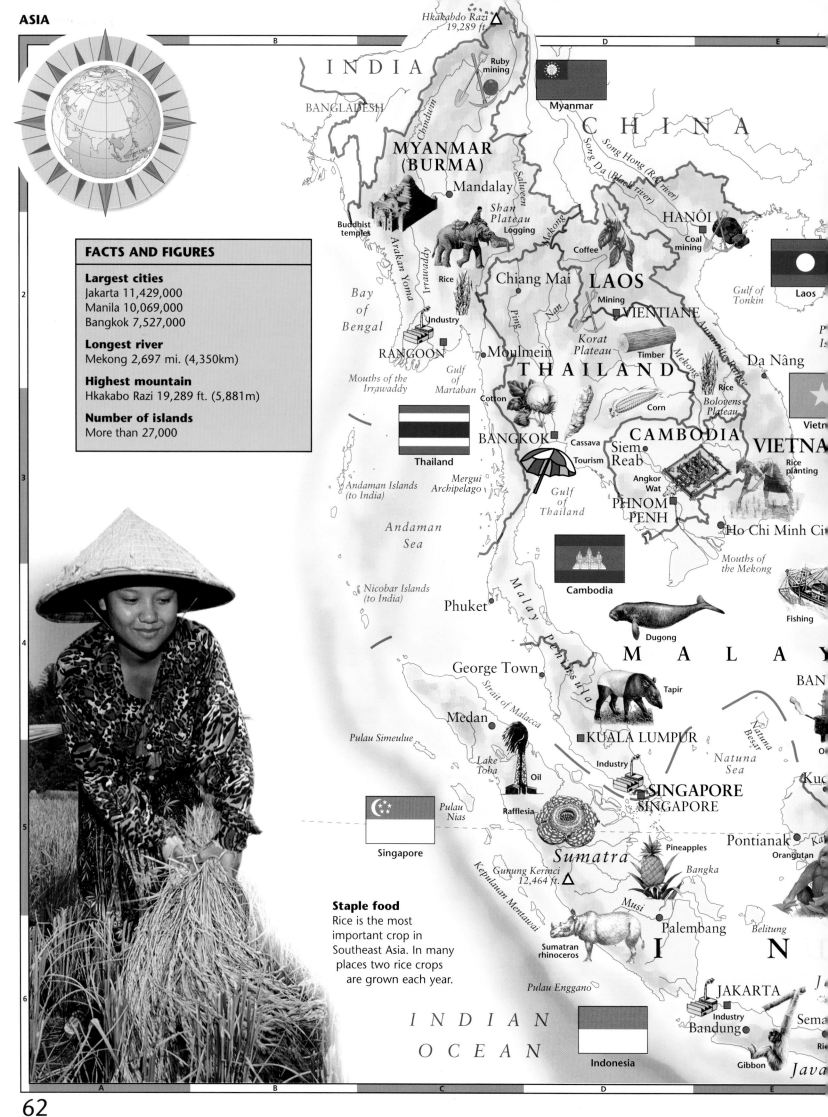

Hkakabdo Razi
19,289 ft △

INDIA

BANGLADESH

Myanmar

CHINA

Ruby
mining

MYANMAR
(BURMA)

Mandalay

Shan
Plateau

Song Da (Black river)

Song Hong (Red river)

HANÔI

Coal
mining

Buddhist
temples

Arakan Yoma

Irrawaddy

Salween

Chindwin

Mekong

Logging

Coffee

Chiang Mai

LAOS

Gulf
of
Tonkin

Laos

Bay
of
Bengal

Rice

Ping

Nan

Mining

VIENTIANE

Korat
Plateau

Timber

Industry

Mekong

Annamite Range

Da Nâng

RANGOON

Moulmein

THAILAND

Rice

Boloyens
Plateau

Vietn

FACTS AND FIGURES

Largest cities
Jakarta 11,429,000
Manila 10,069,000
Bangkok 7,527,000

Longest river
Mekong 2,697 mi. (4,350km)

Highest mountain
Hkakabo Razi 19,289 ft. (5,881m)

Number of islands
More than 27,000

Mouths of the
Irrawaddy

Gulf
of
Martaban

Cotton

Corn

CAMBODIA

VIETNA

Rice

Rice
planting

BANGKOK

Cassava

Thailand

Siem
Reab

Tourism

Mergui
Archipelago

Angkor
Wat

PHNOM
PENH

Gulf
of
Thailand

Ho Chi Minh Ci

Andaman Islands
(to India)

Andaman
Sea

Nicobar Islands
(to India)

Cambodia

Mouths of
the Mekong

Phuket

Malay Peninsula

Fishing

Dugong

MALAY

George Town

Tapir

BAN

Medan

Strait of Malacca

Natuna
Besar

Pulau Simeulue

Lake
Toba

Oil

KUALA LUMPUR

Natuna
Sea

Kuc

Industry

Singapore

Pulau
Nias

Rafflesia

SINGAPORE
SINGAPORE

Pontianak

Ka

Orangutan

Sumatra

Pineapples

Bangka

Musi

Belitung

Staple food
Rice is the most
important crop in
Southeast Asia. In many
places two rice crops
are grown each year.

Gunung Kerinci
12,464 ft △

Kepulauan Mentawai

Sumatran
rhinoceros

Palembang

I

N

Pulau Enggano

JAKARTA

Ja

INDIAN

Industry

Sema

OCEAN

Indonesia

Bandung

Gibbon

Java

Southeast Asia

Located along the equator, Southeast Asia is always hot and often wet, as thunderstorms are common. High mountains and dense forests—home to thousands of unique species of plants and animals—cover much of the land. Beside the great rivers, the Irrawaddy and Mekong, are fertile plains that are important areas for growing rice.

A long, thin strip of land stretches south from Thailand into Malaysia and Singapore. South of there are the region's thousands of islands. Borneo is the third-largest island on Earth. Its land is divided between Malaysia, Indonesia, and Brunei. Brunei is one of the richest countries in the world. Its wealth comes from oil and gas reserves. Indonesia is an island nation. It has more than 13,600 islands, but less than 6,000 of these are inhabited. The Philippines is another island nation made up of around 7,100 islands.

Standing tall
Flooding is common throughout Cambodia, so most people build their homes on stilts above the floodwaters. The walls of these buildings are made out of bamboo, timber, or even palm tree leaves.

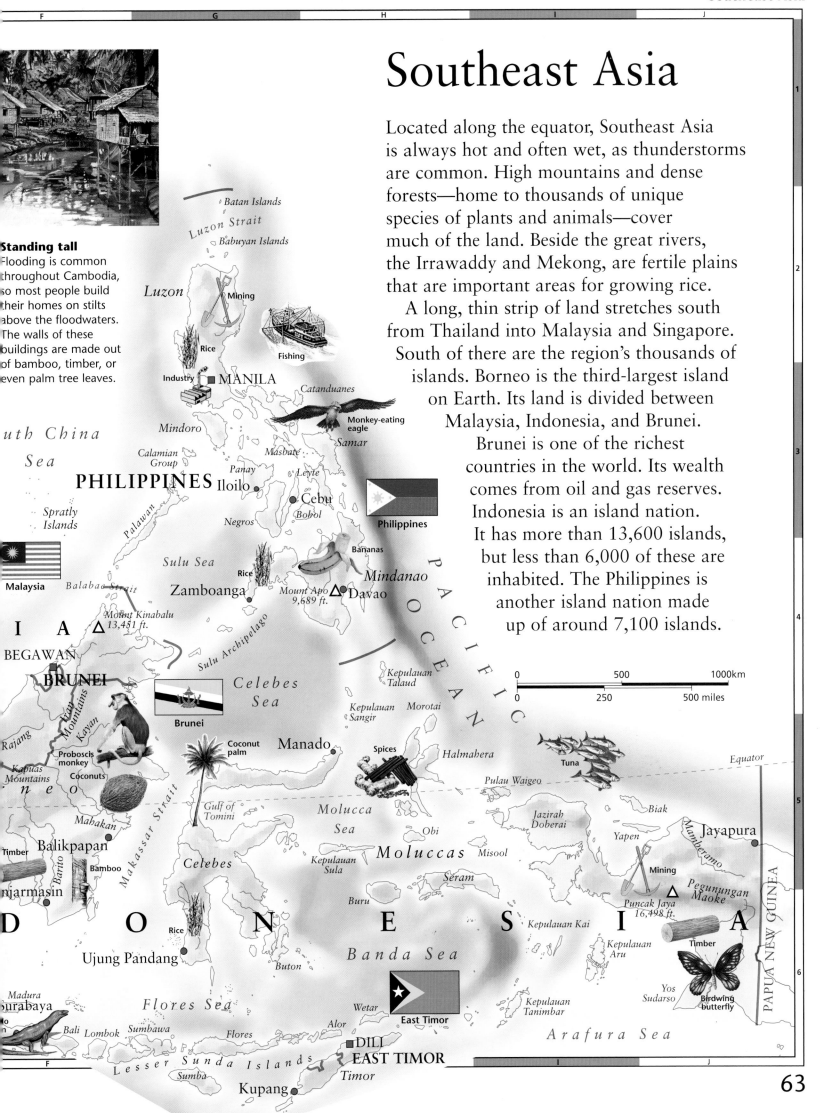

Batan Islands

Luzon Strait

Babuyan Islands

Luzon

Mining

Rice

Fishing

Industry MANILA

Catanduanes

Mindoro

Monkey-eating eagle

South China Sea

Samar

Masbate

Calamian Group

Panay

Leyte

PHILIPPINES Iloilo

Cebu

Bohol

Spratly Islands

Negros

Philippines

Bananas

Sulu Sea

Rice

Mindanao

Malaysia

Zamboanga

Mount Apo 9,689 ft.

Davao

Balabac Strait

Mount Kinabalu 13,451 ft.

I A

Sulu Archipelago

PACIFIC OCEAN

Kepulauan Talaud

BEGAWAN

Celebes Sea

BRUNEI

Kepulauan Sangir

Morotai

Brunei

Iban Mountains

Kayan

Halmahera

Proboscis monkey

Coconut palm

Manado

Spices

Rajang

Tuna

Equator

Kapuas Mountains

Coconuts

Pulau Waigeo

n e o

Mahakan

Gulf of Tomini

Molucca Sea

Jazirah Doberai

Biak

Yapen

Jayapura

Obi

Moluccas

Misool

Timber

Balikpapan

Celebes

Kepulauan Sula

Seram

Mining

Mamberamo

Bamboo

Puncak Jaya 16,498 ft.

Pegunungan Maoke

njarmasin

Barito

Buru

D O N E S I A

Makassar Strait

Kepulauan Kai

Timber

Rice

Kepulauan Aru

Ujung Pandang

Banda Sea

Buton

Yos Sudarso

Birdwing butterfly

Madura

East Timor

Kepulauan Tanimbar

urabaya

Flores Sea

Wetar

PAPUA NEW GUINEA

Bali

Lombok

Sumbawa

Alor

Arafura Sea

Flores

DILI

EAST TIMOR

Lesser Sunda Islands

Timor

Sumba

Kupang

0		500		1000km
0	250		500 miles	

A   B   C   D   E

East Asia

China fills most of East Asia. It is the fourth-largest country in the world and has the highest population—one fifth of the world's people live there. Great rivers, such as the Huang He (Yellow river) and Chang Jiang (Yangtze), flow across the fertile plains. Most of China's industrial cities, as well as the farming regions, are found in the plains since the mountain and desert regions are so inhospitable. The rugged mountains in the southwest are home to the giant panda, which feeds on the bamboo that grows there. In the north lies the Gobi Desert, which crosses the border into Mongolia.

Hong Kong—a major financial center—was returned to Chinese rule in 1997.

Taiwan is a mountainous country. Most of its people live in the west of the island.

FACTS AND FIGURES

Largest cities
Shanghai 9,537,000
Beijing 7,336,000
Hong Kong 6,930,000

Longest river
Chang Jiang (Yangtze) 3,906 mi.
(6,300km)

Highest mountain
Mount Everest 29,021 ft. (8,848m).
This is the highest mountain in the world

Gobi Desert temperatures
Highest 113°F (45°C); lowest -40°F -(40°C)

R U

Olgi

Altay Mountu

Wheat

Oil

Junggar
Basin

KAZAKHSTAN

Urumqi

KYRGYZSTAN

UZBEKISTAN

Tien Shan

Tomur Feng
24,400 ft.

Turpan Pendi
-505 ft.

Tarim He

Kashi

Tarim
Basin

Lop Nur

TAJIKISTAN

Taklimakan Desert

AFGHANISTAN

K2
28,244 ft.

PAKISTAN

(administered
by China, claimed
by India)

Kunlun Shan

Qa

Aksai Chin
(administered
by China, claimed
by India)

Himalayan griffon vulture

Musk deer

Demchok
(administered
by China,
claimed
by India)

Bobak
marmot

Plateau
of Tibet

C

Yak

Red panda

Nu Jian

Siberian ibex

Potala
Palace

Himalayan
black bear

Brahmaputra

Lhasa

NEPAL

Xixabangma Feng
26,282 ft.

Snow
leopard

Mount Everest
29,070 ft.

a   s

BHUTAN

I N D I A

Keep out!
At almost 2,145 mi. (3,460km) long, the Great Wall of China is the world's largest man-made structure. It was built to stop nomadic tribes from invading China.

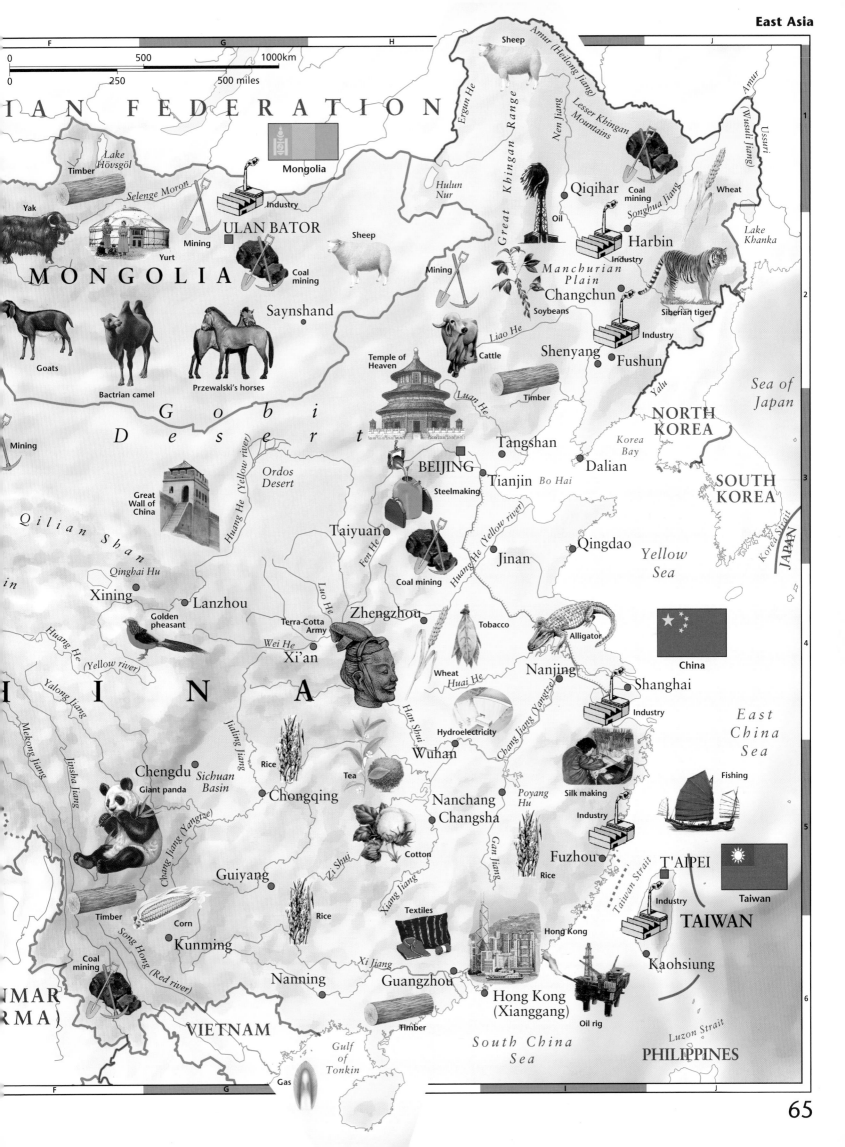

IAN FEDERATION

Timber

Lake Hövsgöl

Selenge Moron

Yak

MONGOLIA

Mongolia

Industry

Mining

ULAN BATOR

Yurt

Coal mining

Saynshand

Sheep

Goats

Bactrian camel

Przewalski's horses

Mining

G o b i D e s e r t

Sheep

Amur (Heilong Jiang)

Ergun He

Nen Jiang

Lesser Khingan Mountains

Great Khingan Range

Hulun Nur

Qiqihar

Coal mining

Oil

Songhua Jiang

Harbin

Industry

Amur (Wusuli Jiang)

Ussuri

Wheat

Lake Khanka

Manchurian Plain

Soybeans

Changchun

Siberian tiger

Industry

Liao He

Shenyang

Fushun

Yalu

Sea of Japan

Mining

Temple of Heaven

Cattle

NORTH KOREA

SOUTH KOREA

JAPAN

Mining

Qilian Shan

Great Wall of China

Ordos Desert

Huang He (Yellow river)

BEIJING

Steelmaking

Luan He

Tangshan

Tianjin   Bo Hai

Dalian

Korea Bay

Qinghai Hu

Xining

Lanzhou

Fen He

Taiyuan

Coal mining

Huang He (Yellow river)

Jinan

Qingdao

Yellow Sea

Korea Strait

Huang He (Yellow river)

Yalong Jiang

Jinsha Jiang

Golden pheasant

Liao He

Zhengzhou

Terra-Cotta Army

Tobacco

Alligator

China

HINA

Wei He

Xi'an

Wheat   Huai He

Nanjing

Shanghai

Industry

East China Sea

Mekong Jiang

Han Shui

Hydroelectricity

Chang Jiang (Yangtze)

Wuhan

Chengdu

Giant panda

Sichuan Basin

Rice

Tea

Nanchang

Changsha

Poyang Hu

Silk making

Industry

Fishing

Chongqing

Cotton

Gan Jiang

Fuzhou

Rice

T'AIPEI

Industry

Taiwan

Zi Shui

Guiyang

Xiang Jiang

Rice

Industry

TAIWAN

Timber

Corn

Kunming

Song Hong (Red river)

Textiles

Xi Jiang

Nanning

Guangzhou

Hong Kong

Hong Kong (Xianggang)

Oil rig

Kaohsiung

Taiwan Strait

Luzon Strait

Coal mining

VIETNAM

Timber

South China Sea

PHILIPPINES

IMAR RMA)

Gulf of Tonkin

Gas

65

Japan and the Koreas

The islands of Japan are mountainous and rugged. Around 3,000 islands form a long chain along the Pacific coast of Asia. The largest and most populated islands are Honshu, Hokkaido, Kyushu, and Shikoku. Japan is in an earthquake zone, and many of the islands are active volcanoes. Buildings need to be able to withstand tremors. The highest of the volcanoes is Fuji san, or Mount Fuji, which last erupted in 1707.

Most of the people of Japan live in bustling cities along the coasts. But Japanese people also love nature and celebrate it in many festivals and ceremonies. In the north of the country the climate is mostly cool, with snow in the winters. Farther south it is milder with hot, humid summers and fierce storms called typhoons in September.

North Korea and South Korea are part of a peninsula of land that stretches into the Sea of Japan. Mountains cover much of both countries. Along the coasts are plains, where most of the people live. Both North and South Korea have cold, snowy winters. The summers are usually hot and wet.

North Korea does not do much trading with other countries, whereas South Korea—like Japan—exports goods all over the world.

Ritual contest
Traditional martial arts are popular in Japan and the Koreas. Kendo, shown here, is a type of fencing that has its origins in the training of the samurai— the warriors of ancient Japan.

CHINA

Coal mining

Hyesan

Ch'ongjin

Rice

Fishing

Steelmaking

Hamhung

Korea Bay

NORTH KOREA

North Korea

PYONGYANG

Songnim

Industry

Kaesong

Paengnyong-do (to South Korea)

SEOUL

Industry

Car manufacturing

Ullung Island

Rice

SOUTH KOREA

Yellow Sea

Electrical goods manufacturing

South Korea

Taegu

Industry

Steelmaking

Pusan

Shipbuilding

Korea Strait

Tsushima

Yamaguc

Higashi suido

△ Halla-san 6,396 ft.

Fukuoka

Kitakyush

Cheju Island

Kuju-san 5,861

Industry

Goto-retto

Kumam

East China Sea

Fukue-jima

Nagasaki

Kyushu

Shipbuilding

Kagoshima

Rice

Sata-misaki

Nansei shoto

Tanega-shi

Yaku-shima

RUSSIAN FEDERATION

La Perouse Strait

Soya-misaki

Rebun-to

Rishiri-to

Macaque

Shiretoko-misaki

Kuril Islands (administered by Russian Federation)

| 0 | 200 | 400km |
| 0 | 100 | 200 miles |

Industry

Asahikawa

△ Taisetsu 7,511 ft.

Kussharo-ko

Hokkaido

FACTS AND FIGURES

Largest cities
Tokyo 29,950,000
(This is the largest city in the world)
Seoul 14,250,000
Osaka 14,190,000

Number of earthquakes
Between 800 and 1,000 each year

Number of volcanoes
Japan has more than 200 volcanoes. Most are extinct (not able to erupt), but 77 are considered active (able to erupt)

Highest mountain
Mount Fuji 12,385 ft. (3,776m)

Car manufacturing

Sapporo

Kushiro

Rice

Factory fishing

Okushiri-to

Uchiura wan

Hakodate

Fishing

Erimo-misaki

Tsugaru Kaikyo

Shimokita-hanto

Mutsu wan

Aomori

Hachinohe

Apples

Fishing

Sardines

Akita

Silka deer

PACIFIC

Fishing

Time for tea
Each aspect of the Japanese tea ceremony is full of meaning. This ritual way of preparing and drinking tea is influenced by Zen Buddhism.

S e a o f

J a p a n

Rice

Sado

Honshu

Sendai

Sendai wan

Niigata

Fukushima

Japan

Dogo

Oki shoto

zen

JAPAN

Noto-hanto

Toyama wan

Toyama

Nagano

Computers

Industry

Hitachi

Kanazawa

Cherry blossoms

Cameras

Tea

Himeji Castle

Wakasa wan

Gifu

Funabashi

Giant salamander

Biwa-ko

Nagoya

TOKYO
Kawasaki
△ *Fuji san 12,385 ft.*

Chiba

Okayama

Industry

Kyoto

Nara

Industry

Motorcycles

Yokohama

Nojima-zaki

Kobe

Sakai

Osaka

Ise wan

Hamamatsu

Hiroshima

Sagami-nada

Izu shoto

Tuna

Bullet train

Citrus fruits

Kii suido

Fishing

atsuyama

ikoku

Tosa wan

Muroto-zaki

Shiono-misaki

PACIFIC

Fishing

OCEAN

ASIA

Federated States of Micronesia

Northern
Mariana
Islands
(to U.S.)

Pagan
Anatahan

Saipan
Tinian

Nauru

Wake Island
(to U.S.)

Johnston Atoll
(to U.S.)

**MARSHALL
ISLANDS**

**Marshall
Islands**

Palau

Guam
(to U.S.)

Yap

KOROR

Babeldaob

Chuuk

PALIKIR
Pohnpei

Caroline Islands

Kusaie

■MAJURO

Tuvalu

Kingman Reef
(to U.S.)

Palmyra Atoll
(to U.S.)

Kiribati

PALAU

**FEDERATED STATES
OF MICRONESIA**

BAIRIKI
■

Gilbert
Islands

Howland Island
(to U.S.)

Baker Island
(to U.S.)

Jarvis Island
(to U.S.)

Admiralty
Islands

New Ireland

NAURU

K I R I B A T I

**PAPUA
NEW
GUINEA**

Bougainville
Island

New
Britain

Santa
Isabel

**SOLOMON
ISLANDS**

TUVALU

Phoenix Islands

**Papu New
Guinea**

New
Georgia
Islands

Guadalcanal

■HONIARA

Malaita

FONGAFALE
■

Tokelau
(to N.Z.)

Northern Cook

SAMOA
Savai'i

American
Samoa
(to U.S.)

Cook
Island
(to N.

PORT MORESBY

San
Cristobal

Santa
Cruz Islands

Wallis
& Futuna
(to France)

SAMOA
Savai'i

APIA
■

Niue
(to N.Z.)

Southern Cook

**Solomon
Islands**

VANUATU

Espiritu Santo

New
Caledonia
(to France)

PORT-VILA
Éfaté

Vanua
Levu

Vitu
Levu

SUVA
■

Lau
Group

TONGA

Kadavu

FIJI

NUKU'ALOFA
■
Tongatapu

Raro

Vanuatu

New
Caledonia

AUSTRALIA

Loyalty Islands

Norfolk Island
(to Australia)

Fiji

Kermadec Islands
(to N.Z.)

Tonga

Samoa

Lord Howe Island
(to Australia)

Australia

■CANBERRA

New Zealand

**NEW
ZEALAND**

■WELLINGTON

Chatham Islands
(to N.Z.)

Tasmania

Bounty Islands
(to N.Z.)

Auckland Islands
(to N.Z.)

Antipodes Islands
(to N.Z.)

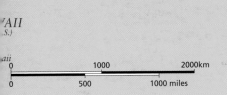

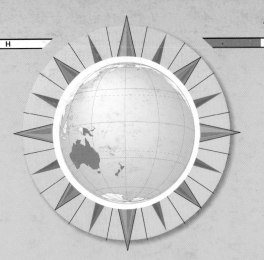

F G H J

'AII
(S.)

aii

0 _____ 1000 _____ 2000km
0 _____ 500 _____ 1000 miles

ati (Christmas Island)

Îles Marquises

Îles Tuamotu

Society Islands

Tahiti

French
Polynesia
(to France)

Gambier
Islands

Pitcairn
Island   Pitcairn
              Islands
              (to U.K.)

Island-hopping
Out of the 330 islands that make up
Fiji, only 106 are inhabited. Scattered
throughout the rest of the region are
more than 20,000 small islands, as
well as much larger ones, including
Australia and New Zealand.

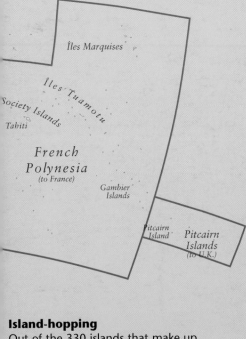

AUSTRALASIA & OCEANIA

Australasia & Oceania is made up of the great landmass of Australia and many thousands of islands in the Pacific Ocean. Australia itself is often described as a continent. Many of the Pacific islands were formed by underwater volcanic eruptions. Coral reefs often grow around these islands. Tropical storms, called typhoons, regularly batter these islands, and the area is also prone to tsunamis— huge waves caused by underwater volcanoes or earthquakes.

The continent is made up of 14 countries: Australia, New Zealand, Papua New Guinea, and several island nations that have become independent in the last 20 years. The rest of the islands are dependencies of other countries.

Flower power
Lush plants and flowers grow in the tropical Cook Islands, and these girls have made traditional flower garlands called leis.

F G H

Australia

Australia is the world's largest island. Its land is mostly flat. The main highland area is the Great Dividing Range in the east of the country. To the west are semiarid plains where only scrubs and grasses grow. Much of western Australia is desert. In the far north there are lush rain forests and mangrove swamps.

Despite its huge size, only around 19.5 million people live in Australia. Most people live in towns and cities along the south and east coasts. The first people in Australia were the aborigines, but the population is now mostly made up of people who migrated to Australia from Europe from the 1700s onward.

Australia is home to many animals that are not found anywhere else on Earth. These include marsupials (mammals that carry their young in pouches) such as kangaroos, wombats, and koalas.

FACTS AND FIGURES

Largest cities
Sydney 3,907,000
Melbourne 3,232,000
Brisbane 1,622,000

Longest river
Murray-Darling 2,325 mi. (3,750km)

Largest lake
Lake Eyre 3,549 sq. mi. (9,100km²). This lake varies in size throughout the year

Highest mountain
Mount Kosciuszko 7,314 ft. (2,230m)

Famous skyline
Sydney's harbor is one of the greatest in the world. The magnificent Sydney Harbour Bridge spans the channel, dividing north and south Sydney. This bridge and the Sydney Opera House are recognized all over the world.

Jumping around
Kangaroo mothers carry their young in a pouch on their bellies. Kangaroos travel by leaping, using their huge back feet.

Melville Island

Van Diemen Gulf

Darwin

Taipan

Arnhem Land

Daly

Wessel Islands

Cape Arnhem

Gulf of Carpentaria

Didgeridoo

Victoria

Baobab tree

Tanami Desert

Lake Woods

Oil

NORTHERN

TERRITORY

Barkly Tableland

Groote Eylandt

Sir Edward Pellew Group

Wellesley Islands

Prince of Wales Island

Cape York

Cape York Peninsula

Princess Charlotte Bay

Cooktown

Cairns

Aboriginal cave paintings

Thorny devil

Sheep shearing

Townsville

Sugarcane

Great Barrier Reef

Coral

Coral Sea

Clown fish

Townshend Island

Beef cattle

Mitchell

Flinders

QUEENSLAND

Coal mining

Rockhampton

Macdonnell Ranges

Alice Springs

Georgina

Uluru (Ayers Rock) 2,844 ft.

Lake Amadeus

Uluru

Simpson Desert

Diamantina

Great Artesian Basin

Thomson

Buckland Tableland

Kookaburra

Bundaberg

Fraser Island

Bactrian camel

Beef cattle

Lake Eyre North

Cooper

Sturt Stony Desert

Sheep

Koalas

Warrego

Dairy cattle

Fishing

SOUTH AUSTRALIA

Lake Eyre South

Lake Blanche

Brisbane

Gold Coast

Mineral Train

Wheat

Lake Torrens

Flinders Ranges

Lake Frome

Darling

Wheat

Duck-billed platypus

Tourism

Lake Everard

Lake Gairdner

Broken Hill

NEW SOUTH WALES

Coal mining

Steelmaking

Great Australian Bight

Port Augusta

Port Pirie

Wine making

Machinery

Newcastle

Sydney Opera House

Seal

Spencer Gulf

York Peninsula

Gulf St. Vincent

Adelaide

Lachlan

Cricket

Murray

Sydney

Wollongong

Australia

INDIAN OCEAN

Kangaroo Island

Fishing

Grapes

Computers

VICTORIA

Cargo ship

Geelong

Melbourne

CANBERRA

AUSTRALIAN CAPITAL TERRITORY

Mount Kosciuszko 7,314 ft.

Great Dividing Range

Cape Howe

Sailing

Tasman Sea

Cape Otway

Bass Strait

South East Point

King Island

Tasmanian devil

Flinders Island

Furneaux Group

Mount Ossa 5,304 ft.

TASMANIA

Hobart

Wombats

T R A L I A

0 400 800km

0 200 400 miles

71

New Zealand

New Zealand is made up of two large islands and several smaller ones. Much of the land is volcanic, and there are many active volcanoes, including Mount Ngaurahoe and Mount Ruapehu on North Island. Hot springs, pools of boiling mud, and geysers are common—especially around Rotorua—and steam from these is used to produce electricity. South Island is dominated by the Southern Alps, which stretch along the western side of the island and are home to the country's highest mountain, Aoraki (Mount Cook), and the Franz Josef Land and Fox glaciers.

New Zealand's fertile lands provide rich pastures for millions of sheep and cattle. In fact, there are more sheep than people living there!

The first people who lived in New Zealand were the Maori—settlers from Polynesia. Throughout the 1800s Europeans began to move there, and they now make up around 90 percent of the population. Most people live in the cities and coastal towns.

North Cape
Rangaunu Bay
Ninety Mile Beach
Sheep
Rugby
Kaipara Harbour
Industry
Great Barrier Island
Hauraki Gulf
Auckland
Manukau Harbour
Coromandel Peninsula
Steelmaking
Waikato
Bay of Plenty
Hamilton
Kiwifruits
North Island
Lake Rotorua
Wheat
Rotorua
Sheep shearing
North Taranaki Bight
Opossums
Lake Taupo
Dairy cattle
Mount Taranaki (Mount Egmont) 8,259 ft.
Cape Egmont
Wanganui
Mount Ngaurahoe 7,514 ft.
Mount Ruapehu 9,174 ft.
Hawke Bay
Mahia Penins
South Taranaki Bight
Kiwi bird
Sheep
Cape Farewell
D'Urville Island
Golden Bay
Tasman Bay
Cook Strait
Karamea Bight
Opossums
Industry
Tourism
Maori art
Wellington
WELLINGTON
Cape Palliser
Cape Foulwind
Tasman Sea
Sheep
South Island
Kaikoura
Southern Alps
Industry
Tourism
Sperm whale
NEW ZEALAND
Franz Josef Glacier
Kiwi bird
Aoraki (Mount Cook) 12,313 ft.
Lake Tekapo
Tuatara
Pegasus Bay
Christchurch
Banks Peninsula
PACIFIC OCEAN
Cascade Point
Canterbury Plains
Lake Ellesmere
Mount Aspiring 9,938 ft.
Wheat
Canterbury Bight
Lake Wanaka
Lake Hawea
Fishing
Tourism
Lake Wakatipu
Queenstown
Yellow-eyed penguin
Lake Te Anau
Roxburgh
Industry
Fiordland
Resolution Island
West Cape
Sheep
Waiau
Dunedin
Otago Peninsula
Albatross
Opossums
Clutha
Dolphin
Mataura
Hydroelectric dam
Foveaux Strait
Seal
South West Cape
Stewart Island

New Zealand

FACTS AND FIGURES

Largest cities
Auckland 1,102,000
Wellington 345,000
Christchurch 331,443

Longest river
Waikato 264 mi. (425km)

Largest lake
Lake Taupo more than 235 sq. mi. (600 km²)

Highest mountain
Aoraki (Mount Cook) 12,313 ft. (3,754m)

0   100   200km
0   50   100 miles

The Poles
The Arctic

The northernmost
and southernmost
points on Earth are called
the poles. Each pole is bitterly
cold and is surrounded by huge ice sheets.
The North Pole floats on an ice sheet in the
Arctic Ocean. The Arctic itself is an area that
includes the North Pole, the Arctic Ocean,
and the most northerly parts of North
America, Europe, and Asia. During the short
summers the Arctic ice sheet shrinks, but in
the winter, when temperatures can fall as low
as -76°F (-60°C), the ice sheet grows again.
Many people live in the lands of the cold
Arctic, including the Inuit, Saami, and
Yugyt. The Arctic is also home to polar
bears, caribou, and walrus.

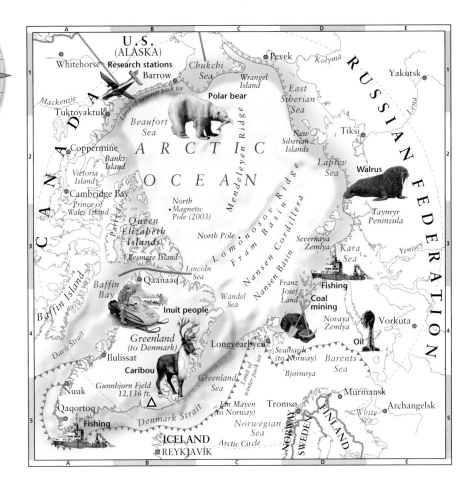

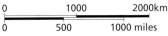

Antarctica

The South Pole
is in Antarctica,
which is the fifth
largest of the seven
continents. Except for
a few sheltered dry valleys
in the mountains, the vast landmass is covered
in snow and ice. Antarctica is the windiest
place on Earth and endures some of the coldest
temperatures. Huge chunks of ice sometimes
break off the ice sheets and form icebergs.
These float in the water, with 90 percent of
their bulk hidden beneath the waves, posing
a danger to ships. There are no countries in
Antarctica, and the only people who live there
are teams of scientists who work at more than
70 research stations that have been set up there.

FACTS AND FIGURES

COUNTRIES AND CAPITALS:
NORTH AMERICA

Antigua & Barbuda	St. John's
Bahamas	Nassau
Barbados	Bridgetown
Belize	Belmopan
Canada	Ottawa
Costa Rica	San José
Cuba	Havana
Dominica	Roseau
Dominican Republic	Santo Domingo
El Salvador	San Salvador
Grenada	St. George's
Guatemala	Guatemala City
Haiti	Port-au-Prince
Honduras	Tegucigalpa
Jamaica	Kingston
Mexico	Mexico City
Nicaragua	Managua
Panama	Panama City
St. Kitts & Nevis	Basseterre
St. Lucia	Castries
St. Vincent & the Grenadines	Kingstown
Trinidad & Tobago	Port of Spain
United States of America	Washington, D.C.

COUNTRIES AND CAPITALS:
SOUTH AMERICA

Argentina	Buenos Aires
Bolivia	La Paz and Sucre
Brazil	Brasília
Chile	Santiago
Colombia	Bogotá
Ecuador	Quito
Guyana	Georgetown
Paraguay	Asunción
Peru	Lima
Suriname	Paramaribo
Uruguay	Montevideo
Venezuela	Caracas

COUNTRIES AND CAPITALS:
EUROPE

Albania	Tirana
Andorra	Andorra la Vella
Austria	Vienna
Belarus	Minsk
Belgium	Brussels
Bosnia & Herzegovina	Sarajevo
Bulgaria	Sofia
Croatia	Zagreb
Czech Republic	Prague
Denmark	Copenhagen
Estonia	Tallinn
Finland	Helsinki
France	Paris
Germany	Berlin
Greece	Athens
Hungary	Budapest
Iceland	Reykjavik
Italy	Rome
Latvia	Riga
Liechtenstein	Vaduz
Lithuania	Vilnius
Luxembourg	Luxembourg
Macedonia	Skopje
Malta	Valletta
Moldova	Chisinâu
Monaco	Monaco
Netherlands	Amsterdam and The Hague
Norway	Oslo
Poland	Warsaw
Portugal	Lisbon
Republic of Ireland	Dublin
Romania	Bucharest
Russian Federation	Moscow
San Marino	San Marino
Serbia & Montenegro	Belgrade
Slovakia	Bratislava
Slovenia	Ljubljana
Spain	Madrid
Sweden	Stockholm
Switzerland	Bern
Ukraine	Kiev
United Kingdom	London
Vatican City	Vatican City

COUNTRIES AND CAPITALS:
AFRICA

Algeria	Algiers
Angola	Luanda
Benin	Porto-Novo
Botswana	Gaborone
Burkina Faso	Ouagadougou
Burundi	Bujumbura
Cameroon	Yaoundé
Cape Verde	Praia
Central African Republic	Bangui
Chad	N'djamena
Comoros	Moroni
Congo	Brazzaville
Democratic Republic of the Congo	Kinshasa
Djibouti	Djibouti
Egypt	Cairo
Equatorial Guinea	Malabo
Eritrea	Asmera
Ethiopia	Addis Ababa
Gabon	Libreville
Gambia, The	Banjul
Ghana	Accra
Guinea	Conakry
Guinea-Bissau	Bissau
Ivory Coast	Yamoussoukro
Kenya	Nairobi
Lesotho	Maseru
Liberia	Monrovia
Libya	Tripoli
Madagascar	Antananarivo
Malawi	Lilongwe
Mali	Bamako
Mauritania	Nouakchott
Mauritius	Port Louis
Morocco	Rabat
Mozambique	Maputo
Namibia	Windhoek
Niger	Niamey
Nigeria	Abuja
Rwanda	Kigali
São Tomé & Príncipe	São Tomé
Senegal	Dakar
Seychelles	Victoria
Sierra Leone	Freetown

Somalia	Mogadishu
South Africa	Pretoria, Bloemfontein and Cape Town
Sudan	Khartoum
Swaziland	Mbabane
Tanzania	Dodoma
Togo	Lomé
Tunisia	Tunis
Uganda	Kampala
Zambia	Lusaka
Zimbabwe	Harare

COUNTRIES AND CAPITALS:

ASIA

Afghanistan	Kabul
Armenia	Yerevan
Azerbaijan	Baku
Bahrain	Manama
Bangladesh	Dhaka
Bhutan	Thimphu
Brunei	Bandar Seri Begawan
Cambodia	Phnom Penh
China	Beijing
Cyprus	Nicosia
East Timor	Dili
Georgia	Tbilisi
India	New Delhi
Indonesia	Jakarta
Iran	Tehran
Iraq	Baghdad
Israel	Jerusalem

(Jerusalem is not recognized by the international community as Israel's capital. Almost all countries treat another city, Tel Aviv, as Israel's capital.)

Japan	Tokyo
Jordan	Amman
Kazakhstan	Astana
Kuwait	Kuwait
Kyrgyzstan	Bishkek
Laos	Vientiane
Lebanon	Beirut

Malaysia	Kuala Lumpur
Maldives	Male
Mongolia	Ulan Bator
Myanmar (Burma)	Rangoon
Nepal	Kathmandu
North Korea	Pyongyang
Oman	Muscat
Pakistan	Islamabad
Philippines	Manila
Qatar	Doha
Russian Federation	Moscow
Saudi Arabia	Riyadh
Singapore	Singapore
South Korea	Seoul
Sri Lanka	Colombo and Sri Jaywardenepura
Syria	Damascus
Taiwan	T'aipei
Tajikistan	Dushanbe
Thailand	Bangkok
Turkey	Ankara
Turkmenistan	Ashgabat
United Arab Emirates	Abu Dhabi
Uzbekistan	Tashkent
Vietnam	Hanoi
Yemen	Sana

COUNTRIES AND CAPITALS:

AUSTRALASIA & OCEANIA

Australia	Canberra
Federated States of Micronesia	Palikir
Fiji	Suva
Kiribati	Bairiki
Marshall Islands	Majuro
Nauru	no capital
New Zealand	Wellington
Palau	Koror
Papua New Guinea	Port Moresby
Samoa	Apia
Solomon Islands	Honiara
Tonga	Nuku'Alofa
Tuvalu	Fongafale
Vanuatu	Port-Vila

LONGEST RIVERS

Nile, Africa	4,135 mi.
Amazon, South America	3,998 mi.
Chang Jiang (Yangtze), Asia	3,906 mi.
Mississippi-Missouri, North America	3,732 mi.
Yenisey-Angara, Asia	3,435 mi.
Huang He (Yellow), Asia	3,388 mi.
Ob-Irtysh, Asia	3,354 mi.
Paraná-Rio de la Plata, South America	3,026 mi.
Congo, Africa	2,914 mi.
Lena, Asia	2,728 mi.

HIGHEST MOUNTAINS

Asia: Mount Everest	29,070 ft.
South America: Aconcagua	22,609 ft.
North America: Mount McKinley	20,320 ft.
Africa: Mount Kilimanjaro	19,335 ft.
Europe: Elbrus	18,506 ft.
Antarctica: Vinson Massif	16,062 ft.
Australasia (Australia and New Zealand): Aoraki (Mount Cook)	12,313 ft.

LARGEST LAKES

Caspian Sea, Asia-Europe	145,000 sq. mi.
Superior, North America	32,117 sq. mi.
Victoria, Africa	27,105 sq. mi.
Huron, North America	23,244 sq. mi.
Michigan, North America	22,542 sq. mi.
Tanganyika, Africa	12,831 sq. mi.
Great Bear, North America	12,400 sq. mi.
Baikal, Asia	11,895 sq. mi.
Malawi, Africa	11,544 sq. mi.
Great Slave, North America	11,115 sq. mi.

The Aral Sea in Asia, once around 25,740 sq. mi. (66,000 km²), is rapidly shrinking

Index

This index lists all the town and city names as well as some of the major physical features on the maps in this atlas. For a city or town the index gives the name and the country in which it is found. For entries that are not cities or towns there is a word in italics describing the type of feature it is. You will find physical features listed under their name rather than their description. For example, Mount Etna appears as "Etna, Mount" in the index.

Each entry gives the number of the page on which the place or feature is found. The letter and number after the page number give the grid square in which you will find it.

A

Aachen Germany 35 B7
Aalborg Denmark 31 B9
Aarhus Denmark 31 B9
Aberdeen United Kingdom 32 D4
Aberystwyth United Kingdom 33 D8
Abha Saudi Arabia 57 F6
Abijan Ivory Coast 48 E5
Abu Dhabi United Arab Emirates 52 B4, 57 I4
Abuja Nigeria 46 B3, 49 F4
Acapulco Mexico 18 E4
Accra Ghana 46 B3, 48 E5
Aconcagua *mountain* 26 C5
Adamaoua *plateau* 49 F5
Adana Turkey 56 E2
Addis Ababa Ethiopia 46 D3, 49 I4
Adelaide Australia 71 G5
Aden Yemen 57 G6
Aden, Gulf of *gulf* 49 J4, 57 G6
Adige *river* 40 D3
Admiralty Islands *islands* 68 B2
Adour *river* 36 E5
Adriatic Sea *sea* 40 E4, 45 A7
Aegean Sea *sea* 45 E8
Afghanistan *country* 52 B4, 59 C8
Africa *continent* 46–51
Africa, Horn of *physical region* 49 J4
Agra India 60 C5
Ahmadabad India 61 B6
Ahvaz Iran 57 H3
Aïr, Massif de L' *mountains* 49 F3
Aix-en-Provence France 37 H6
Ajaccio Corsica 37 J6
Akita Japan 67 H3
Aksai Chin *disputed region* 60 C3, 64 C4
Akureyri Iceland 30 E1
Alabama *river* 17 B8
Alabama *state* U.S. 17 B8
Alakol, Lake *lake* 58 F5
Åland *island* 31 D8
Alaska *state* U.S. 10 B2, 14 B4
Alaska, Gulf of *gulf* 14 B5
Alaska Range *mountains* 14 B4
Albacete Spain 39 G4
Albania *country* 28 D5, 45 B7
Albany Australia 70 D5
Albany New York, U.S. 16 E4
Al Basra Iraq 57 G3
Alberta *province* Canada 12 D4
Albert, Lake *lake* 50 D4
Albuquerque New Mexico, U.S. 15 F4
Aldabra Group *islands* 46 E5, 51 F6
Aldan *river* 55 H3
Aleppo Syria 57 F2
Ålesund Norway 31 A6
Aleutian Islands *islands* 14 A5
Alexandria Egypt 49 H2
Algeria *country* 46 B1, 48 E2
Algiers Algeria 46 B1, 49 F1
Al Hijaz Asir *physical region* 57 F4
Alicante Spain 39 H5
Alice Springs Australia 71 F3
Al Jazirah *physical region* 57 F2
Aller *river* 35 D6
Al Mahrah *mountains* 57 H6
Almaty Kazakhstan 59 E6
Almería Spain 39 G6
Alps *mountains* 37 I5, 40 B2
Altay Mountains *mountains* 55 F5, 58 F4, 64 E1
Altiplano *physical region* 25 F5
Amadeus, Lake *seasonal lake* 71 F3
Amadjuak Lake *lake* 13 H3
Amarillo Texas, U.S. 15 G4
Amazon *river* 24 E3, 25 F3
Amazon Basin *physical region* 25 F2
Amazon, Mouths of the *delta* 25 F2
American Samoa *U.S. dependent territory* 68 E3
Amersfoort the Netherlands 35 B6
Amiens France 37 F1
Amman Jordan 52 A4, 56 E3
Amritsar India 60 B4
Amsterdam the Netherlands 28 B3, 35 B6
Amu Darya *river* 59 C7
Amundsen Gulf *gulf* 12 E2
Amundsen Sea *sea* 73 bottom A4
Amur *river* 55 I5, 65 I1
Anadyr Russian Federation 55 I1
Anchorage Alaska, U.S. 14 B4
Ancona Italy 40 D4
Andaman Islands *islands* 52 C5, 62 C3
Andaman Sea *sea* 62 C3
Andes *mountains* 24 E4, 26 C4
Andorra *country* 28 B4, 39 I1
Andorra la Vella Andorra 28 B4, 39 I2
Andros Island *island* 20 D2
Angara *river* 55 F4
Angel Falls *waterfall* 25 G1
Ångermanälven *river* 31 C6
Angers France 36 E3
Anglesey *island* 33 C7
Angola *country* 46 C5, 51 B7
Angoulême France 36 E4
Anguilla *U.K. dependent territory* 21 I4
Anjouan *island* 51 F7
Ankara Turkey 52 A4, 56 E1
An Nafud *desert* 57 F3
Annamite Range *mountains* 62 E2
Annapolis Maryland, U.S. 17 E6
Annecy France 37 H4
Anse Royal Seychelles 50 F3
Antalya Turkey 56 E2
Antananarivo Madagascar 46 E5, 51 F8
Antarctica *continent* 73 bottom
Antigua *island* 21 I4
Antigua & Barbuda *country* 10 E6, 21 I4
Antipodes Islands *islands* 68 D5
Antofagasta Chile 26 C3
Antwerp Belgium 35 A7
Aomori Japan 67 H2
Aoraki *islands* 72 B5
Apeldoorn the Netherlands 35 B6
Apennines *mountains* 40 C3
Apia Samoa 68 E3
Apo, Mount *volcano* 63 H4
Appalachians *mountains* 17 C7
Apure *river* 25 F1
Aqtau Kazakhstan 59 A6
Arabian Sea *sea* 59 C10, 61 A7
Arafura Sea *sea* 63 I6
Araguaia *river* 25 H3
Aral Sea *inland sea* 59 C6
Archangelsk Russian Federation 54 D2, 73 top E5
Arctic Ocean *ocean* 12 E1, 30 C3, 55 F1, 73 top B2
Arendal Norway 31 A8
Arequipa Peru 24 E4
Argentina *country* 22 B5, 27 D6
Argyle, Lake *salt lake* 71 F2
Arizona *state* U.S. 14 E5
Arkansas *river* 15 I4
Arkansas *state* U.S. 15 H4
Armenia *country* 52 A4, 57 G1
Arnhem the Netherlands 35 B6
Arno *river* Italy 40 C4
Arran *island* 33 C6
Arras France 37 G1
Ar Rub' al Khali *desert* 57 G5
Aruba *Dutch dependent territory* 10 E6, 21 G5
Aruwimi *river* 50 C4
Asahikawa Japan 67 I1
Ascension Island *island* 46 A4
Ashburton *river* 70 C3
Ashgabat Turkmenistan 52 B4, 59 B7
Asia *continent* 52–67
Asir *mountains* 57 F5
Asmera Eritrea 46 D2, 49 I3
Aspiring, Mount *mountain* 72 B5
Astana Kazakhstan 52 B3, 58 D4
Asunción Paraguay 22 C4, 26 E3
Aswân Egypt 49 H2
Asyût Egypt 49 H2
Atacama Desert *desert* 26 C3
Atbara *river* 49 I3
Athabasca *river* 12 D5
Athabasca, Lake *lake* 12 E4
Athens Greece 28 D5, 45 D9
Athlone Republic of Ireland 33 B7
Atlanta Georgia, U.S. 17 C8
Atlantic Ocean *ocean* 13 I3, 17 D8, 21 G2, 25 I5, 27 D8, 30 E2, 33 A9, 35 C4, 38 C6
Atlas Mountains *mountains* 48 D2
Attersee Austria 40 D1
Atyrau Kazakhstan 58 A5
Auckland New Zealand 72 D2
Auckland Islands *islands* 68 D5
Augsburg Germany 35 D9
Augusta Maine, U.S. 16 F4
Austin Texas, U.S. 15 H6
Australasia *continent* 68–71
Australia *country* 68 A4, 70–71
Australian Capital Territory *state* Australia 71 I5
Austria *country* 28 C4, 40 E1
Avignon France 37 H5
Avon *river* 33 D9
Ayers Rock *see* Uluru
Azerbaijan *country* 52 A4, 57 G1
Azov, Sea of *sea* 43 J6

B

Babeldaob *island* 68 A2
Badajoz Spain 38 D4
Baffin Bay *bay* 13 H2, 73 top A3
Baffin Island *island* 13 G2, 73 top A4
Baghdad Iraq 52 A4, 57 G2
Bahamas *country* 10 D5, 20 D2
Bahía Blanca Argentina 27 E6
Bahrain *country* 52 B4, 57 H4
Baikal, Lake *lake* 55 G5
Bairiki Kiribati 68 D2
Baker Island *U.S. dependent territory* 68 D2
Baku Azerbaijan 52 B4, 57 H1
Balaton, Lake *lake* 42 D6
Balearic Islands *islands* 28 B5, 39 I4
Bali *island* 63 F6
Balikpapan Indonesia 63 F5
Balkan Mountains *mountains* 45 D6
Balkhash, Lake *lake* 58 E5
Balsas *river* 18 D4
Baltic Sea *sea* 31 C10, 34 F4, 42 E1
Baltimore Maryland, U.S. 17 D6
Bamako Mali 46 A3, 48 D4
Bandar Seri Begawan Brunei 52 D5, 63 F4
Banda Sea *sea* 63 H6
Bandung Indonesia 62 E6
Bangalore India 61 B8
Bangka *island* 62 D5
Bangkok Thailand 52 D5, 62 D3
Bangladesh *country* 52 C4, 60 E5
Bangui Central African Republic 46 C3, 49 G5
Bangweulu, Lake *lake* 51 D6
Banja Luka Bosnia & Herzegovina 45 B6
Banjarmasin Indonesia 63 F6
Banjul The Gambia 46 A3, 48 C4
Banks Island *island* 12 E2, 73 top A2
Barbados *country* 10 E6, 21 J5
Barbuda *island* 21 I4
Barcelona Spain 39 I2
Barents Sea *sea* 30 F3, 54 E1, 73 top D4
Bari Italy 41 F6
Barito *river* 63 F5
Barkly Tableland *plateau* 71 G2
Barlee, Lake *seasonal lake* 70 D4
Barquisimeto Venezuela 25 F1
Barranquilla Colombia 24 E1
Barre des Ecrins *mountain* 37 H5
Barrow *river* 33 B7
Barrow Alaska, U.S. 73 top B1
Basel Switzerland 40 B1
Basento *river* 41 F6
Basse-Terre *island* 21 I4
Basse-Terre Antigua & Barbuda 21 I4
Basseterre St. Kitts & Nevis 21 I4
Bastia Corsica 37 J5
Bata Equatorial Guinea 50 A4
Bathurst Island *island* 71 F1
Baton Rouge Louisiana, U.S. 15 J5
Bavarian Alps *mountains* 35 E10, 40 C2
Bayonne France 36 E6
Bear *river* 15 F2
Beau Bassin Mauritius 51 F10
Beaufort Sea *sea* 12 D1, 14 C4, 73 top B2
Beijing China 52 D4, 65 H3
Beira Mozambique 51 D8
Beirut Lebanon 52 A4, 56 E2
Belarus *country* 28 D3, 42 F3
Belém Brazil 25 I2
Belfast United Kingdom 33 C6
Belgium *country* 28 B4, 35 A7
Belgrade Serbia & Montenegro 28 D4, 45 C6
Belitung *island* 62 E6
Belize *country* 10 C6, 19 G4
Bellingshausen Sea *sea* 73 A3
Belmopan Belize 10 C6, 19 G4
Belo Horizonte Brazil 25 I5
Belukha, Gora *mountain* 55 F5
Bengal, Bay of *bay* 61 E7, 62 B2
Benghazi Libya 49 G2
Beni *river* 25 F4
Benin *country* 46 B3, 48 E4
Benin, Bight of *bay* 48 E5
Ben Macdhui *mountain* 32 D5
Ben Nevis *mountain* 32 C5
Benue *river* 49 F4
Berezina *river* 43 G3
Bergamo Italy 40 C3
Bergen Norway 31 A7
Bering Sea *sea* 14 A4, 55 J1
Berkner Island *island* 73 bottom B2
Berlin Germany 28 C3, 35 F6
Bermuda *U.K. dependent territory* 10 E5
Bern Switzerland 28 B4, 40 B2
Bernina, Piz *mountain* 40 C2
Besançon France 37 H3
Béticos, Sistemas *mountains* 38 E6
Bhima *river* India 61 B7
Bhopal India 61 C6
Bhutan *country* 52 C4, 60 E5
Bighorn *river* 15 F2
Bighorn Mountains *mountains* 15 F2
Bilbao Spain 39 F1
Bioko *island* 50 A4
Birmingham United Kingdom 33 E8
Birmingham Alabama, U.S. 17 B8
Biscay, Bay of *bay* 36 D4, 38 E1
Bishkek Kyrgyzstan 52 C3, 59 E6
Bismarck North Dakota, U.S. 15 H1
Bissau Guinea-Bissau 48 C4
Bitola Macedonia 45 C7
Bitterroot Range *mountains* 14 E1
Biwa *lake* 67 G5
Bjørnøya *island* 28 D1, 73 top D4
Blackpool United Kingdom 33 D7
Black river *see* Song Hong
Black Sea *sea* 43 H6, 45 F7, 54 B4
Blackwater *river* 33 B8
Blanche, Lake *seasonal lake* 71 G4
Blanc, Mont *mountain* 37 I4, 40 B2
Blantyre Malawi 51 D7
Bloemfontein South Africa 46 D6, 51 C9
Blue Nile *river* 49 I4
Blue Ridge *mountains* 17 C7
Boa Vista *island* 48 C3
Bodø Norway 30 C4
Bogotá Colombia 22 B1, 24 E2
Boise Idaho, U.S. 14 E2
Bolivia *country* 22 B3, 25 F4
Bologna Italy 40 C3
Bolsena, Lago di *lake* 40 C5
Bombay *see* Mumbai
Bonaire *island* 21 G6
Bongo, Massif des *plateau* 49 G4
Bonifacio Corsica 37 J6
Bonn Germany 35 C7
Bordeaux France 36 E5
Borneo *island* 52 D6, 62 E5
Bornholm *island* 31 C10
Bosna *river* 45 B6
Bosnia & Herzegovina *country* 28 C4, 45 B6
Boston Massachusetts, U.S. 16 F4
Bothnia, Gulf of *gulf* 31 D7
Botswana *country* 46 C6, 51 C8
Bougainville Island *island* 68 C3
Boulder Australia 70 E4
Boulogne-sur-Mer France 37 F1
Bounty Islands *islands* 68 D5
Bourges France 37 F3
Bournemouth United Kingdom 33 E9
Bradford United Kingdom 33 E7
Brahmaputra *river* 60 E5, 64 D5
Branco *river* 25 G2
Brasília Brazil 22 D3, 25 I4
Brasov Romania 45 E5
Bratislava Slovakia 28 C4, 43 D5
Bravo del Norte, Río *river* 18 D1 *see also* Grande, Rio
Brazil *country* 22 C2, 25 F3
Brazilian Highlands *physical region* 25 I5
Brazos *river* 15 H5
Brazzaville Congo 46 C4, 50 B5
Brecon Beacons *mountains* 33 D8
Breda the Netherlands 35 A7
Bremen Germany 35 D6
Bremerhaven Germany 34 C5
Brescia Italy 40 C3
Brest Belarus 43 F4
Brest France 36 C2
Bridgetown Barbados 21 J5
Brighton United Kingdom 33 E9
Brisbane Australia 71 J4
Bristol United Kingdom 33 D9
British Colombia *province* Canada 12 D4
British Indian Ocean Territory *U.K. dependent territory* 52 B6
British Virgin Islands *U.K. dependent territory* 21 H3
Brno Czech Republic 42 D5
Broken Hill Australia 71 H4
Brooks Range *mountains* 14 B4
Bruges Belgium 35 A7
Brunei *country* 52 D5, 63 F4
Brussels Belgium 28 B4, 35 A7
Bucharest Romania 28 D4, 45 E6
Buckland Tableland *plateau* 71 I3
Budapest Hungary 28 D4, 42 D6
Buenos Aires Argentina 22 C5, 26 E5
Buffalo New York, U.S. 16 D5
Bug *river* 42 E4
Bujumbura Burundi 46 D4, 50 D5
Bukavu Democratic Republic of the Congo 50 D5
Bulawayo Zimbabwe 51 D8
Bulgaria *country* 28 D5, 45 D7
Bundaberg Australia 71 J3
Burgas Bulgaria 45 E7
Burgos Spain 39 F2
Burkina Faso *country* 46 B3, 48 E4
Burma *see* Myanmar
Buru *island* 63 H6
Burundi *country* 46 D4, 50 D5

C

Cabinda *province* Angola 46 C4, 50 A5
Cáceres Spain 38 E4
Cader Idris *mountain* 33 D8
Cádiz Spain 38 D6
Caen France 36 E2
Cagliari Italy 41 B7
Cairns Australia 71 I2
Cairo Egypt 46 D1, 49 H2
Calais France 37 F1
Calamian Group *islands* 63 G3
Calcutta *see* Kolkata
Calgary Canada 12 D5
Cali Colombia 24 E2
California *state* U.S. 14 D4
California, Gulf of *gulf* 18 B1
Callao Peru 24 E4
Camagüey Cuba 20 D3
Cambodia *country* 52 D5, 62 D3
Cambrian Mountains *mountains* 33 D8
Cambridge United Kingdom 33 F8
Cambridge Bay Canada 73 top A2
Cameroon *country* 46 C3, 49 F5
Campeche, Bay of *bay* 19 F4
Canada *country* 10 C3, 12–13
Canadian *river* 15 G4
Canadian Shield *physical region* 13 F4
Canary Islands *islands* 46 A1, 48 C2
Canberra Australia 68 C4, 71 I5
Cannes France 37 I6
Cantábrica, Cordillera *mountains* 38 D1
Canterbury United Kingdom 33 F9
Canterbury Bight *bay* 72 C5
Canterbury Plains *physical region* 72 C5
Cape Town South Africa 46 C6, 51 B10
Cape Verde *country* 48 C3
Capri *island* Italy 41 E6
Caquetá *river* 24 E2 *see also* Japurá
Caracas Venezuela 22 B1, 25 F1
Carcassonne France 37 F6
Cardiff United Kingdom 33 D9
Cardigan Bay *bay* 33 C8
Carey, Lake *seasonal lake* 70 E4
Caribbean Sea *sea* 21 F5, 24 D1
Caribou Mountains *mountains* 12 E4
Carlisle United Kingdom 33 D6
Carnarvon Australia 70 C3
Carnegie, Lake *seasonal lake* 70 E4
Caroline Islands *islands* 68 B2
Carpathians *mountains* 42 E5, 44 D4
Carpentaria, Gulf of *gulf* 71 G1
Carson City Nevada, U.S. 14 D3
Cartagena Spain 39 H5
Casablanca Morocco 48 E1
Cascade Range *mountains* 14 D2
Caspian Depression *physical region* 58 A5
Caspian Sea *inland sea* 54 C5, 57 H2, 59 A6
Castelló de la Plana Spain 39 H3
Castries St. Lucia 21 J5
Catania Italy 41 E8
Cauca *river* 24 E1
Caucasus *mountains* 54 B4, 57 G1
Cayenne French Guiana 22 D1, 25 H1
Cayman Islands *U.K. dependent territory* 10 D6, 20 C3
Cebu Philippines 63 G3
Cedar *river* 15 I2
Celebes *island* 52 D6, 63 G5
Celebes Sea *sea* 63 G4
Celtic Sea *sea* 33 B9
Central African Republic *country* 46 C3, 49 G4
Central Siberian Plateau *plateau* 55 G3
Central, Sistema *mountains* 38 E3
Ceuta *Spanish dependent territory* 38 E6, 46 B1
Cévennes *mountains* 37 G5
Chad *country* 46 C2, 49 G3
Chad, Lake *lake* 49 G4
Chambal *river* 60 B5
Chamonix France 37 I4
Changchun China 65 I2
Chang Jiang *river* 65 I4
Changsha China 65 H5
Channel Islands *islands* 28 B4, 33 D10
Chapala, Lake *lake* 18 D4
Charente *river* 36 E4
Chari *river* 49 G4
Charleroi Belgium 35 A8
Charleston West Virginia, U.S. 17 C6
Charleston South Carolina, U.S. 17 D8
Charlotte North Carolina, U.S. 17 C7
Charlottetown Canada 13 J5
Chartres France 37 F2
Chatham Islands *islands* 68 D5
Chattahoochee *river* 17 B8
Chattanooga Tennessee, U.S. 17 B7
Chelyabinsk Russian Federation 54 D4
Chemnitz Germany 35 F8
Chenab *river* 59 E8
Chengdu China 65 G5
Chennai (Madras) India 61 C8
Cher *river* 37 F3

Chernivtsi Ukraine 43 F5
Chernobyl Ukraine 43 H4
Cherskiy Range *mountains* 55 H2
Chesapeake Bay *inlet* 17 E6
Cheyenne *river* 15 G2
Cheyenne Wyoming, U.S. 15 G3
Chiang Mai Thailand 62 C2
Chiba Japan 67 H5
Chicago Illinois, U.S. 16 B5
Chico *river* 27 D7, 27 D9
Chiemsee *lake* 35 E10
Chihuahua Mexico 18 D2
Chile *country* 22 B6, 27 C6
Chimborazo *mountain* 24 D2
China *country* 52 C4, 64 E4
Chindwin *river* 62 C1
Chiriqui, Golfo de *gulf* 19 I6
Chisinău Moldova 28 D4, 43 G6
Chita Russian Federation 55 H5
Chittagong Bangladesh 61 E6
Ch'ongjin South Korea 67 E2
Chongqing China 65 G5
Christchurch New Zealand 72 C5
Chubut *river* 27 D7
Chukchi Sea *sea* 14 A4, 73 top B1
Churchill *river* 13 F4
Cincinnati Ohio, U.S. 17 C6
Ciudad Juárez Mexico 18 D1
Clermont-Ferrand France 37 G4
Cleveland Ohio, U.S. 16 C5
Cluj-Napoca Romania 44 D5
Clyde *river* 33 D6
Coast Mountains *mountains* 12 C3
Coast Ranges *mountains* 14 C2
Coco *river* 19 H5
Coimbatore India 61 B8
Coimbra Portugal 38 C3
Cologne Germany 35 B7
Colombia *country* 22 B1, 24 E2
Colombo Sri Lanka 52 C5, 61 C9
Colorado *river* (Argentina) 27 C6
Colorado *river* (Mexico/U.S.) 14 E5, 15 F3
Colorado *river* (Texas, U.S.) 15 H5
Colorado *state* U.S. 15 F4
Colorado Plateau *plateau* 14 E4
Columbia *river* 14 D1
Columbia South Carolina, U.S. 17 C7
Columbia Plateau *plateau* 14 E2
Columbus Ohio, U.S. 17 C6
Como, Lago di *lake* 40 C2
Comoros *country* 46 E5, 51 F6
Conakry Guinea 46 A3, 48 D4
Concepción Chile 27 C6
Conchos *river* 18 C2
Concord New Hampshire, U.S. 16 E4
Congo *country* 46 C4, 50 B5
Congo *river* 50 B5
Congo Basin *physical region* 50 B4
Congo, Democratic Republic of the *country* 46 C4, 50 B5
Connecticut *state* U.S. 16 E5
Constance, Lake *lake* 35 C10, 40 C1
Constanta Romania 45 F6
Constantine Algeria 49 F1
Cook Islands *N.Z. dependent territory* 68 E3
Cook, Mount *see* Aoraki
Cooktown Australia 71 H2
Cooper *seasonal river* 71 G4
Copenhagen Denmark 28 C3, 31 B10
Coppermine Canada 73 top A2
Coral Sea *sea* 71 J2
Córdoba Argentina 26 D5
Córdoba Spain 38 E5
Corfu *island* 45 C8
Corinth Greece 45 D9
Cork Republic of Ireland 33 B8
Corno Grande *mountain* 40 D5
Coropuna, Nevado *mountain* 24 E4
Corrib, Lough *lake* 33 A7
Corsica *island* 28 B5, 37 J6
Costa Rica *country* 10 C6, 19 H6
Cotopaxi *volcano* 24 D2
Cotswold Hills *hills* 33 E8
Coventry United Kingdom 33 E8
Cowan, Lake *seasonal lake* 70 E5
Craiova Romania 45 D6
Crete *island* 28 D6, 45 E10
Crete, Sea of *sea* 45 E10
Creuse *river* 37 F3
Croatia *country* 28 C4, 44 A5
Cuando *river* 51 B7
Cuango *river* 51 B6
Cuanza *river* 51 B6
Cuba *country* 10 D5, 20 D2
Cubango *river* 51 B8
Cúcuta Colombia 24 E1
Culiacán Mexico 18 C3
Curaçao *island* 21 G6
Curitiba Brazil 25 H6
Cusco Peru 24 E4
Cyclades *islands* 45 D9
Cyprus *country* 52 A4, 56 E2
Czech Republic *country* 28 C4, 42 C5

D

Dakar Senegal 46 A2, 48 C3
Dalälven *river* 31 C8
Dalian China 65 I3
Dallas Texas, U.S. 15 I5
Daly *river* 71 F1
Damascus Syria 52 A4, 56 E2
Damavand, Qolleh-ye *mountain* 57 H2
Da Nâng Vietnam 62 E2
Danube *river* 35 D10, 40 E1, 42 D6, 45 E6
Danube Delta *delta* 45 F5
Danzig, Gulf of *gulf* 42 D3
Dar es Salaam Tanzania 51 E6
Darien, Golfo de *gulf* 19 J6, 24 E1
Darling *river* 71 H4
Darmstadt Germany 35 C8
Dart *river* 33 D9
Dartmoor *moorland* 33 D9
Darwin Australia 71 F1
Daugavpils Latvia 43 F2
Davao Philippines 63 H4
Death Valley *valley* 14 D4
Deccan *plateau* 61 B6
Dee *river* 32 D5
Delaware *state* U.S. 17 E6
Delhi India 60 C4
Demchok *disputed region* 60 C3, 65 C4
Denmark *country* 28 C3, 31 A10
Denver Colorado, U.S. 15 G3
Derby Australia 70 E2
Derby United Kingdom 33 E8
Derry *see* Londonderry
Deseado *river* 27 D8
Des Moines Iowa, U.S. 15 I3
Des Moines *river* 15 I3
Desna *river* 43 H4
Desventurados, Islas de los *islands* 22 A4
Detroit Michigan, U.S. 16 C5
Dhaka Bangladesh 52 C4, 60 E5
Dhawlagiri *mountain* 60 D4
Diamantina *seasonal river* 71 G3
Dieppe France 37 F1
Dijon France 37 H3
Dili East Timor 52 E6, 63 H6
Dinaric Alps *mountains* 45 B6
Disappointment, Lake *seasonal lake* 70 D3
Djibouti *country* 46 E3, 49 I4
Djibouti Djibouti 46 E3, 49 J4
Dnieper *river* 43 G3
Dniester *river* 43 G5
Dnipropetrovs'k Ukraine 43 I5
Dodecanese *islands* 45 E9
Dodoma Tanzania 46 D4, 51 E6
Doha Qatar 52 B4, 57 H4
Dolomites *mountains* 40 D2
Dominica *country* 10 E6, 21 I5
Dominican Republic *country* 21 G3, 10 D6
Don *river* (Russian Federation) 54 C3
Don *river* (United Kingdom) 32 D4
Donegal Bay *bay* 33 A6
Donets *river* 43 I4
Donets'k Ukraine 43 J5
Dordogne *river* 37 F5
Dordrecht the Netherlands 35 A7
Dortmund Germany 35 C7
Dos Hermanas Spain 38 E5
Douglas Isle of Man 33 C7
Douro *river* 38 D3
Dover United Kingdom 33 F9
Dover Delaware, U.S. 17 E6
Dovrefjell *plateau* 31 B7
Drakensberg *mountains* 51 C10
Drau *river* 40 D2
Drava *river* 40 E2, 42 D6, 44 B5
Dresden Germany 35 F7
Drina *river* 45 C6
Dubai United Arab Emirates 57 I4
Dubawnt Lake *lake* 13 F4
Dublin Republic of Ireland 28 B3, 33 C7
Dubrovnik Croatia 45 B7
Duero *river* 39 F2
see also Douro
Dufourspitze *mountain* 40 B2
Dumont d'Urville Sea *sea* 73 bottom D5
Dundee United Kingdom 32 D5
Dunedin New Zealand 72 C6
Dunkerque France 37 F1
Durance *river* 37 H5
Durban South Africa 51 D10
D'Urville Island *island* 72 D3
Dushanbe Tajikistan 52 B4, 59 D7
Düsseldorf Germany 35 B7

E

East China Sea *sea* 65 J4, 66 C6
Eastern Ghats *mountains* 61 C8
East Falkland *island* 27 E9
East Frisian Islands *islands* 34 C5
East London South Africa 51 C10
East Siberian Sea *sea* 55 H1, 73 top D1
East Timor *country* 52 E6, 63 H6
Ebro *river* 39 G2
Ecuador *country* 22 A2, 24 D2
Edinburgh United Kingdom 32 D5
Edmonton Canada 12 E5
Edward, Lake *lake* 50 D5
Egmont, Mount *see* Taranaki, Mount
Egypt *country* 46 D2, 49 H2
Eindhoven the Netherlands 35 B7
El Aaiùn Western Sahara 46 A1, 48 D2
Elba *island* 40 C4
Elbe *river* 34 D5, 42 C4
Elbert, Mount *mountain* 15 F3
Elbrus *mountain* 54 B4
Elburz Mountains *mountains* 57 H2
Elde *river* 34 E5
El Gîza Egypt 49 H2
Ellesmere Island *island* 13 G1, 73 top B3
Ellesmere, Lake *lake* 72 C5
El Obeid Sudan 49 H4
El Paso Texas, U.S. 15 F5
El Salvador *country* 10 E6, 19 G5
Elx Spain 39 H5
Emmen the Netherlands 35 C6
Ems *river* Germany 35 C6
England *national region* United Kingdom 33 D7
English Channel *channel* 33 D10, 36 D1
Enns *river* 40 D1
Enschede the Netherlands 35 C6
Equatorial Guinea *country* 46 B4, 50 A4
Erfurt Germany 35 E7
Ergun He *river* 65 H1
Erie, Lake *lake* 13 H6, 16 C5
Eritrea *country* 46 D2, 49 I3
Erzgebirge *mountains* 35 E8
Esbjerg Denmark 31 A10
Esfahan Iran 57 H3
Espiritu Santo *island* 68 C3
Espoo Finland 31 E8
Essen Germany 35 C7
Essequibo *river* 25 G2
Estonia *country* 28 D3, 43 F1
Ethiopia *country* 46 D3, 49 I5
Ethiopian Highlands *mountains* 49 I4
Etna, Mount *volcano* 41 E8
Eugene Oregon, U.S. 14 D2
Euphrates *river* 57 G3
Europe *continent* 28–45
Everard, Lake *seasonal lake* 71 G4
Everest, Mount *mountain* 60 D5, 64 D5
Everglades, The *wetland* 17 D10
Evros *river* 45 E7
Exe *river* 33 D9
Exeter United Kingdom 33 D9
Exmouth Gulf *gulf* 70 C3
Eyre North, Lake *seasonal lake* 71 G4
Eyre South, Lake *seasonal lake* 71 G4

F

Faroe Islands *Danish dependent territory* 28 B2
Fair Isle *island* 32 E3
Faisalabad Pakistan 59 E9
Falkland Islands *U.K. dependent territory* 22 C6, 27 E9
Faro Portugal 38 D5
Fen He *river* 65 H3
Ferrara Italy 40 D3
Fès Morocco 48 E1
Fiji *country* 68 D3
Finland *country* 28 D2, 31 E7
Finland, Gulf of *gulf* 31 E8
Finsteraarhorn *mountain* 40 B2
Fitzroy *river* 70 E2
Flinders *river* 71 H2
Flinders Island *island* 71 I6
Florence Italy 40 C4
Flores Sea *sea* 63 G6
Florida *state* U.S. 17 C9
Florida Keys *islands* 17 C10
Foggia Italy 40 E5
Fongafale Tuvalu 68 D3
Formentera *island* 39 I4
Fortaleza Brazil 25 J3
Fort-de-France Martinique 21 J5
Forth, Firth of *inlet* 32 D5
Fort Lauderdale Florida, U.S. 17 D10
Fort Peck Lake *lake* 15 F1
Fort William United Kingdom 32 C5
Fort Worth Texas, U.S. 15 H5
Foxe Basin *sea* 13 G3
France *country* 28 B4, 36–37
Frankfort Kentucky, U.S. 17 B6
Frankfurt am Main Germany 35 C8
Franz Josef Land *islands* 55 F1, 73 top D4
Fraser *river* 12 D5
Fraser Island *island* 71 J4
Fredericton Canada 13 I6
Freeport Bahamas 20 D1
Freetown Sierra Leone 46 A3, 48 D4
Freiburg im Breisgau Germany 35 C10
Fremantle Australia 70 D5
French Guiana *French dependent territory* 22 D1, 25 H2
French Polynesia *French dependent territory* 69 F4
Fresno California, U.S. 14 D4
Frisian Islands *islands* 34 B5
Frome, Lake *seasonal lake* 71 G4
Fuerte *river* 18 C2
Fuji san *mountain* 67 H5
Fukue-jima *island* 66 D6
Fukuoka Japan 66 E5
Fukushima Japan 67 H4
Fulda *river* 35 D8
Funabashi Japan 67 H5
Furneaux Group *islands* 71 I6
Fushun China 65 I2
Fuzhou China 65 I5

G

Gabon *country* 46 C4, 50 A5
Gaborone Botswana 46 D6, 51 C9
Gairdner, Lake *seasonal lake* 71 G5
Galapágos Islands *islands* 24 D5
Galati Romania 44 F5
Galdhopiggen *mountain* 31 B7
Galway Republic of Ireland 33 A7
Gambia, The *country* 46 A3, 48 C4
Gambier Islands *islands* 69 F4
Gandhi Sagar *lake* 60 B5
Ganges *river* 60 D5
Ganges, Mouths of the *delta* 61 E6
Gan Jiang *river* 65 I5
Garda, Lago di *lake* 40 C3
Garonne *river* 36 E5
Garoua Cameroon 49 F4
Gävle Sweden 31 C7
Gdansk Poland 42 D3
Geelong Australia 71 H6
Geneva Switzerland 40 A2
Geneva, Lake *lake* 37 I4, 40 A2
Genoa Italy 40 B3
Georgetown Guyana 22 C1, 25 G1
George Town Malaysia 62 D4
Georgia *country* 52 A3, 57 F1
Georgia *state* U.S. 17 C8
Georgian Bay *bay* 13 H6, 16 C4
Georgina *seasonal river* 71 G3
Gera Germany 35 E7
Geraldton Australia 70 C4
Gerlachovsky Stit *mountain* 42 E5
Germany *country* 28 C4, 35 D7
Ghaghra *river* 60 D5
Ghana *country* 46 B3, 48 E4
Ghent Belgium 35 A7
Gibraltar *U.K. dependent territory* 28 A5, 38 E6
Gibson Desert *desert* 70 E3
Gifu Japan 67 G5
Gijón Spain 38 E1
Gila *river* 14 E5
Gilbert Islands *islands* 68 D2
Girona Spain 39 J2
Gironde *estuary* 36 E4
Glåma *river* 31 B7
Glasgow United Kingdom 32 D5
Glittertind *mountain* 31 B7
Gloucester United Kingdom 33 D8
Gobi Desert *desert* 65 G3
Godavari *river* 61 C7
Goiânia Brazil 25 H4
Gold Coast Australia 71 J4
Gonder Ethiopia 49 I4
Göteborg (Gothenburg) Sweden 31 B9
Gotland *island* 28 D3, 31 D9
Goto-retto *islands* 66 D6
Göttingen Germany 35 D7
Gozo *island* 41 D9
Grampian Mountains *mountains* 32 C5
Granada Spain 39 F5
Gran Canaria *island* 48 C2
Grand Bahama *island* 20 D1
Grand Canyon *canyon* 14 E4
Grand Cayman *island* 20 E3
Grand Comore *island* 51 F7
Grande, Rio *river* (Brazil) 25 I5
Grande, Rio *river* (U.S./Mexico) 15 G5, 18 D1
see also Bravo del Norte, Río
Grande-Terre *island* 21 I4
Grand River *river* 15 G2
Gran Paradiso *mountain* 40 B3
Granville Lake *lake* 13 F5
Graz Austria 40 E2
Great Australian Bight *bay* 71 F5
Great Barrier Island *island* 72 D1
Great Barrier Reef *reef* 71 H1
Great Basin *physical region* 14 D3
Great Bear Lake *lake* 12 E3
Great Dividing Range *mountains* 71 H5
Greater Antarctica *plateau* 73 bottom D3
Greater Antilles *islands* 20 C3
Great Hungarian Plain *physical region* 42 E6
Great Ouse *river* 33 F8
Great Plains *physical region* 12 E5, 15 G1
Great Rift Valley *valley* 49 I5, 50 D4, 50 E4
Great Salt Lake *salt lake* 14 E3
Great Salt Lake Desert *physical region* 14 E3
Great Sandy Desert *desert* 70 D2
Great Slave Lake *lake* 12 E4
Great Victoria Desert *desert* 70 E4
Greece *country* 28 D5, 45 C8
Greenland *Danish dependent territory* 10 D1, 73 top B4
Greenland Sea *sea* 73 top C5
Grenada *country* 10 E6, 21 I6
Grenadines, The *islands* 21 J5
Grenoble France 37 H4
Groningen the Netherlands 34 B5
Grossglockner *mountain* 40 D2
Guadalajara Mexico 18 D4
Guadalcanal *island* 68 C3
Guadalquivir *river* 38 E5
Guadeloupe *French dependent territory* 21 J4
Guadiana *river* 38 D5, 39 F4
Guam *U.S. dependent territory* 68 B1
Guangzhou China 65 H6
Guaporé *river* 25 G4
Guatemala *country* 10 C6, 19 G5
Guatemala City Guatemala 10 C6, 19 G5
Guaviare *river* 25 F2
Guayaquil Ecuador 24 D3
Guernsey *island* 33 D10
Guiana Highlands *physical region* 25 F1
Guinea *country* 46 A3, 48 D4
Guinea-Bissau *country* 46 A3, 48 C4
Guiyang China 65 G5
Gujranwala Pakistan 59 E9
Gulf, The *gulf* 57 H3
Gunnbjørn Fjeld *mountain* 73 top B5
Guyana *country* 22 C1, 25 G1

H

Haarlem the Netherlands 35 A6
Hachinohe Japan 67 I3
Hadramawt *mountains* 57 H6
Hague, The the Netherlands 28 B3, 35 A6
Hainan *island* 52 D5, 65 H6
Haiti *country* 10 D6, 21 F3
Hakodate Japan 67 H2
Halifax Canada 13 J6
Halla-san *mountain* 66 D5
Halle Germany 35 E7
Halmahera *island* 63 H5
Hamamatsu Japan 67 G5
Hamburg Germany 34 D5
Hamhung North Korea 66 D3
Hamilton Canada 13 H6
Hamilton New Zealand 72 D2
Hannover Germany 35 D6
Hanoi 52 D5, 62 E2
Han Shui *river* 65 H4
Harare Zimbabwe 46 D5, 51 D8
Harbin China 65 I2
Harris *island* 32 B4
Harrisburg Pennsylvania, U.S. 16 D5
Hartford Connecticut, U.S. 16 E5
Hauraki Gulf *gulf* 72 D1
Havana Cuba 10 D5, 20 C2
Havel *river* 35 E6
Hawaii *island* 14 B6
Hawaii *state* U.S. 14 B5
Hawea, Lake *lake* 72 B5
Heidelburg Germany 35 C9
Heilong Jiang *see* Amur
Helena Montana, U.S. 15 F1
Helgoländer Bucht *bay* 34 C5
Helmand *river* 59 C9
Helsingborg Sweden 31 B10
Helsinki Finland 28 D2, 31 E8
Herat Afghanistan 59 C8
Hiiumaa *island* 42 E1
Himalayas *mountains* 60 B3, 64 C4
Hindu Kush *mountains* 59 D8
Hiroshima Japan 67 F5
Hispaniola *island* 21 F3
Hitachi Japan 67 H4
Hkakabo Razi *mountain* 62 C1
Hobart Australia 71 H6
Ho Chi Minh City Vietnam 62 E3
Hokkaido *island* 52 E3, 67 I1
Holyhead United Kingdom 33 C7
Homyel Belarus 43 H3
Honduras *country* 10 C6, 19 G5
Honduras, Golfo de *gulf* 19 G4
Hong Kong China 65 I6
Honiara Solomon Islands 68 C3
Honolulu Hawaii, U.S. 14 B5
Honshu *island* 52 E4, 67 H4
Houston Texas, U.S. 15 I6
Hövsgol, Lake *lake* 65 F1
Howland Island *U.S. dependent territory* 68 D2
Huai He *river* 65 H4
Huang He *river* 65 F4
Huascarán Nevado *mountain* 24 E3
Hudson Bay *bay* 13 G4
Huelva Spain 38 D5
Hulun Nur *lake* 65 H1
Humber *river* 33 E7
Humboldt *river* 14 D3
Hungary *country* 28 C4, 42 D6
Huron, Lake *lake* 13 H6, 16 C4
Hvannadalshnúkur *mountain* 30 F2
Hyderabad India 61 C7
Hyderabad Pakistan 59 D10
Hyères, Îles d' *islands* 37 H6
Hyesan North Korea 66 D2

I

Iasi Romania 44 E4
Ibérico, Sistema *mountains* 39 G3
Ibiza *island* 28 B5, 39 I4
Iceland *country* 28 B1, 30 E1, 73 top B5
Idaho *state* U.S. 14 E2
Ijsselmeer *lake* 35 B6
Ile *river* 59 E6
Illampu *mountain* 25 F4
Illinois *river* 16 A5
Illinois *state* U.S. 17 A6
Iloilo Philippines 63 G3
Ilulissat Greenland 73 top A4
Inarijärvi *lake* 30 E3
India *country* 52 C5, 60 B5
Indiana *state* U.S. 17 B6
Indianapolis Indiana, U.S. 17 B6
Indian Ocean *ocean* 51 F9, 57 I6, 61 C10, 62 C6, 70 C2, 71 F5, 73 bottom D1
Indigirka *river* 55 H2
Indonesia *country* 52 D6, 62 D6
Indore India 61 B6
Indus *river* 59 E8, 60 C3
Indus, Mouths of the *delta* 59 D10
Inland Sea *sea* 67 F5
Inn *river* 40 C2
Inner Hebrides *islands* 32 B5
Innsbruck Austria 40 D2
Interlaken Switzerland 40 B2
Inverness United Kingdom 32 D4
Ionian Islands *islands* 45 C8
Ionian Sea *sea* 41 F8, 45 B9
Iowa *state* U.S. 15 I3
Ipel *river* 42 D5
Ipswich United Kingdom 33 F8
Iqaluit Canada 13 H3
Iraklion Greece 45 E10
Iran *country* 52 B4, 57 H2
Iranian Plateau *plateau* 57 I3
Iraq *country* 52 A4, 57 F2
Ireland, Republic of *country* 28 A3, 33 B7
Iriri *river* 25 H3
Irish Sea *sea* 33 C7
Irkutsk Russian Federation 55 G5
Irrawaddy *river* 62 C2
Irrawaddy, Mouths of the *delta* 62 C2
Irtysh *river* 54 E4
Isabela, Isla *island* 24 D6
Isar *river* 35 E9
Ischia *island* 41 D6
Isère *river* 37 H4
Ise-wan *straight* 67 G5
Ishim *river* 58 C4
Iskar *river* 45 D6
Islamabad Pakistan 52 C4, 59 E8
Islay *island* 32 C5
Isle *river* 36 E5
Ismoili Somoni, Qullai *mountain* 59 D7
Isole Eolie *islands* 41 E7
Israel *country* 52 A4, 56 E3
Istanbul Turkey 56 D1
Italy *country* 28 C5, 40 C4
Ivory Coast *country* 46 A3, 48 D4
Izmir Turkey 56 D1
Izu shoto *islands* 67 H5

J

Jabalpur India 61 C6
Jackson Mississippi, U.S. 17 A8

Jacksonville Florida, U.S. 17 C9
Jaffna Sri Lanka 61 C9
Jaipur India 60 B5
Jakarta Indonesia 52 D6, 62 E6
Jalalabad Afghanistan 59 D8
Jamaica *country* 10 D6, 20 D4
James *river* 15 H2
James Bay *bay* 13 H5
Jammu and Kashmir *political region* 60 B3
Jan Mayen Island *island* 28 C1, 73 top C5
Japan *country* 52 E4, 67 F4
Japan, Sea of *sea* 67 F3
Japurá *river* 25 F2
Jarvis Island *U.S. dependent territory* 68 E2
Java *island* 52 D6, 62 E6
Java Sea *sea* 62 E6
Jaya, Puncak *mountain* 63 J6
Jayapura Indonesia 63 J5
Jebel Toubkal *mountain* 48 D2
Jeddah Saudi Arabia 57 F5
Jefferson City Missouri, U.S. 15 I3
Jeju-do *island* 66 C5
Jerez de la Frontera Spain 38 E6
Jersey *island* 33 D10
Jerusalem Israel 52 A4, 56 E3
Jhelum *river* 59 E8
Jialing Jiang *river* 65 G4
Jinan China 65 I3
Jinsha Jiang *river* 65 F5
Johannesburg South Africa 51 C9
Johnston Atoll *U.S. dependent territory* 68 E1
Jönköping Sweden 31 C9
Jordan *country* 52 A4, 57 F3
Jostedalsbreen *glacier* 31 A7
Jotunheimen *mountains* 31 A7
Juan Fernández Island *island* 22 A5
Júcar *river* 39 G4
Julian Alps *mountains* 40 D2
Juneau Alaska, U.S. 14 C4
Junggar Basin *physical region* 64 E2
Jura *island* 32 C5
Jura *mountains* 37 H4
Juruá *river* 24 E3
Juruena *river* 25 G4
Jutland *peninsula* 31 A9
Juventud, Isla de la *island* 20 C2

K

K2 *mountain* 59 E8, 64 C3
Kabul Afghanistan 52 B4, 59 D8
Kadavu *island* 68 D3
Kaesong North Korea 66 D3
Kagoshima Japan 66 E6
Kaikoura New Zealand 72 D4
Kalahari Desert *desert* 51 B9
Kalémié Democratic Republic of the Congo 51 D6
Kalgoorlie Australia 70 E4
Kaliningrad Russian Federation 42 E3, 55 C2
Kalixälven *river* 30 E5
Kalmar Sweden 31 C9
Kampala Uganda 46 D4, 50 D4
Kananga Democratic Republic of the Congo 51 C6
Kanazawa Japan 67 G4
Kandahar Afghanistan 59 C9
Kangaroo Island *island* 71 G5
Kano Nigeria 49 F4
Kanpur India 60 C5
Kansas *state* U.S. 15 H3
Kansas City Kansas, U.S. 15 I3
Kaohsiung Taiwan 65 J6
Kapuas *river* 62 E5
Karachi Pakistan 58 D10
Karakoram Range *mountains* 59 E8
Karakum *desert* 59 B7
Karakum Canal *canal* 59 B7
Kara Sea *sea* 54 E2, 73 top D3
Kariba, Lake Zambia 51 C7
Karlsruhe Germany 35 C9
Kárpathos *island* 45 F10
Karun *river* 57 H3
Kasai *river* 50 B5
Kashi China 64 C3
Kassel Germany 35 D7
Kathmandu Nepal 52 C4, 60 D5
Kauai *island* 14 A5
Kaunas Lithuania 43 F2
Kawasaki Japan 67 H5
Kayan *river* 63 F5
Kazakhstan *country* 52 B3, 58 C5
Kazakh Uplands *physical region* 58 D5
Kazan Russian Federation 54 D3
Kazbek *mountain* 57 G1
Kea, Mauna *mountain* 14 B6
Kebnekaise *mountain* 30 D4
Kefallinia *island* 45 C9
Keflavík Iceland 30 E2
Keitele *lake* 31 E6
Kemi Finland 30 E5
Kemijoki *river* 30 E5
Kentucky *state* U.S. 17 B6
Kenya *country* 46 D4, 50 E4
Kenya, Mount *mountain* 50 E5
Kepulauan Aru *islands* 63 I6
Kepulauan Kai *islands* 63 I6
Kepulauan Mentawai *islands* 62 C5
Kepulauan Sula *islands* 63 H5
Kepulauan Tanimbar *islands* 63 I6
Kerch Ukraine 43 J6
Kerinci, Gunung *mountain* 62 D5
Kermadec Islands *N.Z. dependent territory* 68 D4
Khabarovsk Russian Federation 55 I4
Khambhat, Gulf of *gulf* 61 A6
Khanka, Lake *lake* 65 J2
Kharkiv Ukraine 43 I4
Khartoum Sudan 46 D2, 49 H3
Kiel Germany 34 D5
Kieler Bucht *bay* 34 D4
Kiev Ukraine 28 D4, 43 H4
Kifisos *river* 45 D9
Kigali Rwanda 46 D4, 50 D5
Kilimanjaro, Mount *mountain* 50 E5
Killarney Republic of Ireland 33 A8
Kimberley South Africa 51 C9
Kimberley Plateau *plateau* 70 E2
Kinabalu, Mount *mountain* 63 F4
King Island *island* 71 H6
Kingman Reef *U.S. dependent territory* 68 E2
Kingston Canada 13 H6
Kingston Jamaica 10 D6, 20 E4
Kingston-upon-Hull United Kingdom 33 E7
Kingstown St. Vincent & the Grenadines 21 I5
Kinshasa Democratic Republic of the Congo 46 C4, 50 B5
Kirgiz Range *mountains* 59 D6
Kirgiz Steppe *physical region* 58 C5
Kiribati *country* 68 D2
Kirkenes Norway 30 F3
Kirkwall United Kingdom 32 D3
Kirov Russian Federation 54 D3
Kiruna Sweden 30 D4
Kisangani Democratic Republic of the Congo 50 C4
Kismaayo Somalia 49 I5
Kisumu Kenya 50 E5
Kitakyushu Japan 66 E5
Kitwe Zambia 51 D7
Kivu, Lake *lake* 50 D5
Klaipeda Lithuania 42 E2
Klarälven *river* 31 C8
Kliuchevskoi *volcano* 55 J3
Kobe Japan 67 G5
Koblenz Germany 35 C8
Kodiak Island *island* 14 B5
Kolkata India 61 E6
Kolyma *river* 55 I2, 73 top D1
Kolyma Range *mountains* 55 I2
Korab *mountain* 45 C7
Korat Plateau *plateau* 62 D2
Korea Bay *bay* 65 I3, 66 C3
Korea Strait *channel* 66 D5
Korhogo Ivory Coast 48 D4
Korinthiakos Kolpos *gulf* 45 D9
Koror Palau 68 B2
Kosciuszko, Mount *mountain* 71 I5
Kosice Slovakia 42 E5
Kotuj *river* 55 G2
Kraków Poland 42 E5
Krasnoyarsk Russian Federation 55 F4
Krefeld Germany 35 B7
Krishna *river* 61 B7
Kristiansand Norway 31 A8
Krk *island* 44 A5
Kuala Lumpur Malaysia 52 D5, 62 D4
Kuching Malaysia 62 E5
Kuju-san *mountain* 66 E6
Kula Kangri *mountain* 60 E4
Kumamoto Japan 66 E6
Kumasi Ghana 48 E5
Kunlun Shan *mountains* 64 D4
Kunming China 65 G6
Kuopio Finland 31 F6
Kupang Indonesia 63 G6
Kuril Islands *islands* 53 F2, 55 J3, 67 J1
Kushiro Japan 67 I1
Kussharo-ko *lake* 67 I1
Kutch, Gulf of *gulf* 61 A6
Kutch, Rann of *physical region* 59 D10, 60 A5
Kuwait *country* 52 A4, 57 G3
Kuwait Kuwait 52 B4, 57 G3
Kwilu *river* 50 B5
Kyoto Japan 67 G5
Kyrgyzstan *country* 52 B3, 59 E6
Kyushu *island* 66 E6

L

Labrador Sea *sea* 13 H3
Laccadive Islands *islands* 52 B5, 60 A8
Lachlan *river* 71 H5
La Coruña Spain 38 D1
Ladoga, Lake *lake* 54 C2
Lågen *river* 31 B7
Lagos Nigeria 48 E5
Lagos Portugal 38 C5
Lahore Pakistan 59 E9
Lake District *physical region* 33 D6
Lakonikos Kolpos *gulf* 45 D10
La Marmora, Punta *mountain* 41 B6
Lansing Michigan, U.S. 16 B5
Lanzarote *island* 48 D2
Lanzhou China 65 G4
Laos *country* 52 D5, 62 D2
La Paz Bolivia 22 B3, 25 F4
La Paz Mexico 18 C3
La Plata Argentina 26 E5
Laptev Sea *sea* 55 G2, 73 top D2
La Rochelle France 36 E4
Las Palmas Canary Islands 48 D2
Las Vegas Nevada, U.S. 14 E4
Latvia *country* 28 D3, 43 F2
Lau Group *islands* 68 D3
Laurentian Highlands *physical region* 13 I5
Lausanne Switzerland 40 A2
Lausitzer Neisse *river* 35 F7
Lebanon *country* 52 A4, 56 E2
Leeds United Kingdom 33 E7
Leeuwarden the Netherlands 34 B5
Leeward Islands *islands* 21 H3
Le Havre France 36 E2
Leicester United Kingdom 33 E8
Leiden the Netherlands 35 A6
Leipzig Germany 35 E7
Le Mans France 36 E3
Lena *river* 55 G4, 73 top E1
Lens France 37 G1
León Mexico 18 D3
León Spain 38 E2
Lepontine Alps *mountains* 40 B2
Lerwick United Kingdom 32 E2
Lesbos *island* Greece 45 E8
Lesina, Lago di *lagoon* 40 E5
Lesotho *country* 46 D6, 51 C10
Lesser Antarctica *physical region* 73 bottom B3
Lesser Antilles *islands* 21 G5
Lesser Sunda Islands *islands* 63 F6
Lewis *island* 32 C4
Lhasa China 64 E5
Liao He *river* 65 I2
Liberia *country* 46 A3, 48 D5
Libreville Gabon 46 C4, 50 A4
Libya *country* 46 C2, 49 G2
Libyan Desert *desert* 49 G2
Liechtenstein *country* 28 C4, 40 C2
Liège Belgium 35 B8
Liffey *river* 33 C7
Ligurian Sea *sea* 40 B4
Likasi Democratic Republic of the Congo 51 C6
Lille France 37 G1
Lillehammer Norway 31 B7
Lilongwe Malawi 46 D5, 51 D7
Lima Peru 22 A3, 24 E4
Limerick Republic of Ireland 33 B8
Limnos *island* 45 E8
Limoges France 37 F4
Limpopo *river* 51 C8
Linares Spain 39 F5
Lincoln Nebraska, U.S. 15 H3
Lincoln Sea *sea* 73 top B3
Line Islands *islands* 68 E2
Linköping Sweden 31 C9
Linz Austria 40 E1
Lion, Golfe de *gulf* 37 G6
Lippe *river* 35 C7
Lisbon Portugal 28 A5, 38 C4
Lithuania *country* 28 D3, 42 E2
Little Colorado *river* 15 F4
Little Missouri *river* 15 G2
Little Rock Arkansas, U.S. 15 I4
Liverpool United Kingdom 33 D7
Livojoki *river* 30 E5
Livorno Italy 40 C4
Ljubljana Slovenia 28 C4, 40 E2
Ljusnan *river* 31 C7
Llivia Spain 39 I2
Loa, Mauna *mountain* 14 B6
Lodz Poland 42 E4
Lofoten *islands* 28 C1, 30 C4
Logan, Mount *mountain* 12 C3
Loire *river* 36 D3, 37 G3
Lomani *river* 50 C5
Lomé Togo 46 B3, 48 E5
Lomond, Loch *lake* 32 D5
London United Kingdom 28 B3, 33 E9
London Canada 13 H6
Londonderry United Kingdom 33 B6
Long Island *island* 16 E5
Longyearbyen Svalbard 73 top C4
Lop Nur *seasonal lake* 64 E3
Lord Howe Island *island* 68 C4
Lorient France 36 D3
Los Angeles California, U.S. 14 D4
Lot *river* 37 F5
Louisiana *state* U.S. 15 I5
Louisville Kentucky, U.S. 17 B6
Lourdes France 36 E6
Lower Lough Erne *lake* 33 B6
Lower Tunguska *river* 55 F3
Loyalty Islands *islands* 68 C3
Lualuba *river* 50 C5
Luanda Angola 46 C4, 51 A6
Luan He *river* 65 H3
Lubango Angola 51 A7
Lübeck Germany 34 D5
Lubumbashi Democratic Republic of the Congo 51 C6
Lucerne Switzerland 40 B2
Lucknow India 60 C5
Lugano Switzerland 40 B2
Lukenie *river* 50 B5
Luleå Sweden 30 D5
Luleälven *river* 30 D5
Luo He *river* 65 H4
Lusaka Zambia 46 D5, 51 D7
Lut, Dasht-e *desert* 57 I3
Luton United Kingdom 33 E8
Luxembourg *country* 28 B4, 35 B8
Luxembourg Luxembourg 28 B4, 35 B8
Luzon *island* 52 D5, 63 G2
L'viv Ukraine 43 F5
Lyon France 37 H4

M

Maas *river* 35 B7
see also Meuse
Maastricht the Netherlands 35 B7
McClintock Channel *channel* 13 F2
MacDonnell Ranges *mountains* 71 F3
Macedonia *country* 28 D5, 45 C7
Mackay, Lake *seasonal lake* 71 F3
Mackenzie *river* 12 D3, 73 top A1
Mackenzie Mountains *mountains* 12 D3
McKinley, Mount *mountain* 14 B4
Macleod, Lake *lake* 70 C3
Madagascar *country* 46 E6, 51 F7
Madeira *Portuguese dependent territory* 46 A1, 48 D1
Madeira *river* 25 G3
Mädelegabel *mountain* 35 D10
Madison Wisconsin, U.S. 16 A5
Madras *see* Chennai
Madre de Dios *river* 25 F4
Madrid Spain 28 A5, 39 F3
Madurai India 61 C9
Magadan Russian Federation 55 I3
Magdalena *river* 24 E1
Magdeburg Germany 35 E6
Maggiore, Lago *lake* 40 B2
Mahajanga Madagascar 51 F7
Mahakan *river* 63 F5
Mahanadi *river* 61 D6
Maiduguri Nigeria 49 F4
Main *river* 35 D8
Main-Donau-Kanal *canal* 35 E9
Maine *state* U.S. 16 F3
Maine, Gulf of *gulf* 16 F4
Mainland *island* 32 D3
Mainland *island* 32 E2
Mainz Germany 35 C8
Majorca *island* 28 B5, 39 I4
Majuro Marshall Islands 68 D2
Malabo Equatorial Guinea 46 B3, 50 A4
Málaga Spain 39 F6
Malaita *island* 68 C3
Mälaren *lake* 31 E8
Malawi *country* 46 D5, 51 D7
Malawi (Nyasa), Lake *lake* 51 E7
Malaysia *country* 52 D5, 62 D4
Maldives *country* 52 B5, 61 B10
Male Maldives 52 B5, 61 B10
Malheur Lake *lake* 14 D2
Mali *country* 46 B2, 48 E3
Malmö Sweden 31 B10
Malta *country* 28 C5, 41 D9
Malta *island* 41 E9
Malta Channel *channel* 41 D9
Mamberamo *river* 63 J5
Mamoré *river* 25 F4
Manado Indonesia 63 H5
Managua Nicaragua 10 C6, 19 H5
Manamah Bahrain 52 B4, 57 H4
Manaus Brazil 25 G3
Manchester United Kingdom 33 D7
Manchurian Plain *physical region* 65 I2
Mandalay Myanmar 62 C1
Manila Philippines 52 D5, 63 G3
Man, Isle of *island* 28 B3, 33 C7
Manitoba *province* Canada 13 F5
Manitoba, Lake *lake* 13 F5
Mannar, Gulf of *gulf* 61 C9
Mannheim Germany 35 C9
Maoke, Pegunungan *mountains* 63 J5
Maputo Mozambique 46 D6, 51 D9
Maracaibo Venezuela 24 E1
Maracaibo, Lago *lake* 24 E1
Marajó *island* 25 H2
Marañón *river* 24 E3
Marbella Spain 38 E6
Mar Chiquita, Laguna *lake* 26 E4
Mar del Plata Argentina 27 E6
Margow, Dasht-e *desert* 59 C9
Maribor Slovenia 40 E2
Maritime Alps *mountains* 37 I5
Maritsa *river* 45 E7
Mariupol' Ukraine 43 J5
Markermeer *lake* 35 B6
Marmara Denizi *sea* 45 F7
Marmolada *mountain* 40 D2
Marne *river* 37 H2
Marquises, Îles *islands* 69 F4
Marrakech Morocco 48 D1
Marsala Italy 41 D8
Marseille France 37 H6
Marshall Islands *country* 68 C1
Martaban, Gulf of *gulf* 62 C2
Martha's Vineyard *island* 16 F5
Martinique *French dependent territory* 21 I5
Mary Turkmenistan 59 C7
Maryland *state* U.S. 17 E6
Masai Steppe *physical region* 50 E5
Maseru Lesotho 46 D6, 51 C9
Mashhad Iran 57 I2
Massachusetts *state* U.S. 16 E5
Massif Central *plateau* 37 G4
Matadi Democratic Republic of the Congo 50 A5
Mataura *river* 72 B6
Matsuyama Japan 67 F5
Matterhorn *mountain* 40 B2
Maturín Venezuela 25 G1
Maui *island* 14 B6
Mauritania *country* 46 A2, 48 D3
Mauritius *country* 46 E5, 51 F9
Mayotte *French dependent territory* 46 E5, 51 F7
Mazar-e Sharif Afghanistan 59 D8
Mbabane Swaziland 46 D6, 51 D9
Mbandaka Democratic Republic of the Congo 50 B5
Mbeya Tanzania 51 D6
Mbuji-Mayi Democratic Republic of the Congo 51 C6
Mead, Lake *lake* 14 E4
Mecca Saudi Arabia 57 F5
Mecklenburger Bucht *bay* 34 E5
Medan Indonesia 62 C4
Medellín Colombia 24 E1
Medicine Hat Canada 12 E5
Medina Saudi Arabia 57 F4
Mediterranean Sea *sea* 37 H6, 39 I5, 41 A6, 45 E10, 49 G1, 56 D2
Mekong Jiang *river* 62 D2, 65 F4
Mekong, Mouths of the *delta* 62 E3
Melbourne Australia 71 H6
Melilla *Spanish dependent territory* 46 B1
Melville Island *island* 71 F1
Memphis Tennessee, U.S. 17 A7
Mendoza Argentina 26 C5
Mérida Mexico 19 G3
Messina Italy 41 E7
Messiniakos Kolpos *gulf* 45 D10
Meta *river* 24 E1
Metz France 37 H2
Meuse *river* 35 B7, 37 H2
see also Maas
Mexicali Mexico 18 B1
Mexico *country* 10 B5, 18 D3
Mexico City Mexico 10 B5, 18 E4
Mexico, Gulf of *gulf* 15 I6, 17 B9, 19 F2, 20 B1
Miami Florida, U.S. 17 D10
Michigan *state* U.S. 16 B5
Michigan, Lake *lake* 13 G6, 16 B4
Micronesia, Federated States of *country* 68 B2
Middlesbrough United Kingdom 33 E6
Midi, Canal du *canal* 37 F6
Mikkeli Finland 31 F7
Milan Italy 40 C3
Milk *river* 15 F1
Milwaukee Wisconsin, U.S. 16 B5
Mindanao *island* 52 D5, 63 H4
Mindoro *island* 63 G3
Minneapolis Minnesota, U.S. 15 I2
Minnesota *river* 15 I2
Minnesota *state* U.S. 15 H1
Miño *river* 38 D2
Minorca *island* 28 B5, 39 J3
Minsk Belarus 28 D3, 43 G3
Mirtóon Pélagos *sea* 45 D9
Mississippi *river* 15 I2 & J4, 16 A4
Mississippi *state* U.S. 17 A8
Mississippi Delta *delta* 15 J6, 17 A9
Missouri *river* 15 H3
Missouri *state* U.S. 15 I4
Mitchell *river* 71 H2
Mittellandkanal *canal* 35 C6
Mjøsa *lake* 31 B7
Mobile Alabama, U.S. 17 B9
Modena Italy 40 C3
Mogadishu Somalia 46 E4, 49 J5
Mohéli *island* 51 F7
Mojave Desert *desert* 14 D4
Moldova *country* 28 D4, 43 G6
Molokai *island* 14 B6
Moluccas *islands* 52 E6, 63 H5
Molucca Sea *sea* 63 H5
Mombasa Kenya 50 E5
Monaco *country* 28 B4, 37 I5
Monaco Monaco 37 I5
Mönchen-gladbach Germany 35 B7
Mongolia *country* 52 D3, 65 F2
Monrovia Liberia 46 A3, 48 D5
Montana *state* U.S. 15 F1
Montego Bay Jamaica 20 D4
Monterrey Mexico 18 E2
Montevideo Uruguay 22 C5, 26 F5
Montgomery Alabama, U.S. 17 B8
Montpelier Vermont, U.S. 16 E4
Montpellier France 37 G6
Montreal Canada 13 I6
Montserrat *U.K. dependent territory* 21 I4
Monza Italy 40 C3
Moore, Lake *seasonal lake* 70 D4
Morava *river* 42 D5
Morena, Sierra *mountains* 38 D5
Morocco *country* 46 B1, 48 D1
Moroni Comoros 46 E5, 51 F7
Mortes *river* 25 H4
Moscow Russian Federation 28 E3, 54 C3
Mosel *river* 35 C8
see also Moselle
Moselle *river* 35 B8, 37 H2
see also Mosel
Mosquitos, Golfo de los *gulf* 19 I6
Mostar Bosnia & Herzegovina 45 B6
Mosul Iraq 57 G2
Moulmein Myanmar 62 C2
Mount Isa Australia 71 G2
Moyynqum *desert* 59 D6
Mozambique *country* 46 D6, 51 D8
Mozambique Channel *channel* 51 E8
Mulhacén *mountain* 39 F6
Mulhouse France 37 I3
Mull *island* 32 C5
Multan Pakistan 58 D9
Mumbai India 61 B7
Munich Germany 35 E10
Munku-Sardyk, Gora *mountain* 55 G5
Münster Germany 37 C7
Könkamaälven *river* 30 D4
Mur *river* 40 E2
Murcia Spain 39 G5
Mures *river* 44 D5
Müritz *lake* 34 E5
Murmansk Russian Federation 54 D2, 73 top D5
Murray *river* 71 H5
Musala *mountain* 45 D7
Muscat Oman 52 B4, 57 J4
Musi *river* Indonesia 62 D5
Mutare Zimbabwe 51 D8
Mwanza Tanzania 50 D5
Mweru, Lake *lake* 51 D6
Myanmar *country* 52 C4, 62 C1

N

Naga Hills *hills* 60 F5
Nagano Japan 67 H4
Nagasaki Japan 66 E6
Nagoya Japan 67 G5
Nagpur India 61 C6
Nagpur, Chota *plateau* 61 D6
Nairobi Kenya 46 D4, 50 E5
Namib Desert *desert* 51 A8
Namibia *country* 46 C5, 51 B8
Nampula Mozambique 51 E7
Namsen *river* 31 C6
Namur Belgium 35 A8
Nan *river* 62 D2
Nanchang China 65 I5
Nancy France 37 H2
Nanga Parbat *mountain* 59 E8
Nanjing China 65 I4
Nanning China 65 H6
Nantes France 36 E3
Nantucket Island *island* 16 F5
Naples Italy 41 E6
Napo *river* 24 E2
Nara Japan 67 G5
Narew *river* 42 E3
Narmada *river* 61 B6
Narodnaya, Gora *mountain* 54 E3
Narvik Norway 30 D4
Nashville Tennessee, U.S. 17 B7
Nassau Bahamas 10 D5, 20 D1
Nasser, Lake *lake* 49 H3

Natal Brazil 25 J3
Natuna Besar *islands* 62 E4
Natuna Sea *sea* 62 E5
Nauru *country* 68 C2
Navassa Island *U.S. dependent territory* 20 E4
N'djamena Chad 46 C3, 49 G4
Ndola Zambia 51 D7
Neagh, Lough *lake* 33 C6
Nebitdag Turkmenistan 59 B7
Nebraska *state* U.S. 15 G3
Neckar *river* 35 D9
Negro *river* 25 F2
Negro, Río *river* 27 D6
Negros *island* 63 G3
Nelson *river* 13 F5
Neman *river* 42 E2
Nen Jiang *river* 65 I1
Nepal *country* 52 C4, 60 C4
Ness, Loch *lake* 32 D4
Netherlands, the *country* 28 B3, 34 B6
Netherlands Antilles *Dutch dependent territory* 10 E6, 21 G6 & I4
Nettilling Lake *lake* 13 H3
Neuchâtel, Lac de *lake* 40 A2
Neusiedler See *lake* 40 F1
Nevada *state* U.S. 14 D3
Nevada, Sierra *mountains* 39 F6
Nevis *island* 21 I4
New Britain *island* 68 C3
New Brunswick *province* Canada 13 I5
New Caledonia *French dependent territory* 68 C3
New Caledonia *island* 68 C3
Newcastle Australia 71 I5
Newcastle-upon-Tyne United Kingdom 33 E6
New Delhi India 52 C4, 60 C4
Newfoundland *island* 13 J5
Newfoundland & Labrador *province* Canada 13 I4
New Georgia Islands *islands* 68 C3
New Hampshire *state* U.S. 16 E4
New Ireland *island* 68 C2
New Jersey *state* U.S. 16 E5
Newman Australia 70 D3
New Mexico *state* U.S. 15 F5
New Orleans Louisiana, U.S. 15 J6
New Siberian Islands *islands* 52 E1, 55 G2, 73 top D2
New South Wales *state* Australia 71 H4
New York New York, U.S. 16 E5
New York *state* U.S. 16 D4
New Zealand *country* 68 C4, 72 E4
Ngauruhoe, Mount *mountain* 72 D3
Niagara Falls *waterfall* 16 D4
Niamey Niger 46 B3, 48 E4
Nicaragua *country* 10 C6, 19 H5
Nicaragua, Laguna de *lake* 19 H6
Nice France 37 I5
Nicobar Islands *islands* 52 C5, 61 F9, 62 C4
Nicosia Cyprus 52 A4, 56 E2
Niger *country* 46 B2, 49 F3
Niger *river* 48 E4
Nigeria *country* 46 B3, 49 F4
Niigata Japan 67 H4
Nijmegen the Netherlands 35 B7
Nile *river* 49 H3
Nîmes France 37 G5
Niobrara *river* U.S. 15 G2
Nipigon, Lake *lake* 13 G6
Nis Serbia & Montenegro 45 C6
Niue *N.Z. dependent territory* 68 E3
Nizhniy Novgorod Russian Federation 54 D3
Nord-Ostsee-Kanal *canal* 34 D5
Norfolk Virginia, U.S. 17 E6
Norfolk Island *Australian dependent territory* 68 D4
Norrköping Sweden 31 C8
North America *continent* 10–21
Northampton United Kingdom 33 E8
North Carolina *state* U.S. 17 D7
North Dakota *state* U.S. 15 G1
Northern Cook Islands *islands* 68 E3
Northern Dvina *river* 54 D2
Northern Ireland *national region* United Kingdom 33 B6
Northern Mariana Islands *U.S. dependent territory* 68 B1
Northern Sporades *islands* 45 D8
Northern Territory *state* Australia 71 F2
North European Plain *physical region* 42 D3, 54 D3
North Frisian Islands *islands* 34 C4
North Island *island* 72 D2
North Korea *country* 52 E4, 66 D3
North Magnetic Pole *pole* 73 top B3
North Platte *river* 15 G3
North Pole *pole* 73 top C3
North Saskatchewan *river* 12 E5
North Sea *sea* 31 A9, 33 F6, 34 B5
North Uist *island* 32 B4
Northwest Highlands *mountains* 32 C5
Northwest Territories *province* Canada 12 D3
North York Moors *moorland* 33 E6
Norway *country* 28 C3, 31 B7
Norwegian Sea *sea* 30 B4, 73 top C5
Norwich United Kingdom 33 F8
Nottingham United Kingdom 33 E8
Nouakchott Mauritania 46 A2, 48 C3
Novara Italy 40 B3
Nova Scotia *province* Canada 13 J5
Novaya Zemlya *islands* 54 E2, 73 top D4
Novi Sad Serbia & Montenegro 44 C5
Novokuznetsk Russian Federation 55 F4
Novosibirsk Russian Federation 55 F4
Nubian Desert *desert* Sudan 49 I3
Nu Jiang *river* 64 E4
see also Salween
Nuku'Alofa Tonga 68 D3
Nunavut *province* Canada 13 F3
Nunivak Island *island* 14 B4
Nuremberg Germany 35 E9
Nuuk Greenland 10 E2, 73 top A5

O

Oahu *island* 14 B5
Ob *river* 54 E3
Oban United Kingdom 32 C5
Odense Denmark 31 B10
Oder *river* 35 F6, 42 D4
Oderhaff *bay* 34 F5
Odesa Ukraine 43 H6
Ogbomosho Nigeria 48 E4
Ohio *river* 17 C6
Ohio *state* U.S. 17 C6
Ohrid, Lake *lake* 45 C8
Oise *river* 37 G1
Ojos del Solado, Nevado *mountain* 26 C4
Okavango Delta *delta* 51 B8
Okayama Japan 67 F5
Okeechobee, Lake *lake* 17 C10
Okhotsk, Sea of *sea* 55 I3
Oklahoma *state* U.S. 15 H4
Oklahoma City Oklahoma, U.S. 15 H4
Okushiri-to *island* 67 H2
Öland *island* 28 C3, 31 C9
Oldenburg Germany 35 C6
Olekma *river* 55 H4
Olenek *river* 55 G2
Olgiy Mongolia 64 E1
Olt *river* 45 D6
Olympia Washington, U.S. 14 D1
Olympus *mountain* 45 D8
Olympus, Mount *mountain* 14 D1
Omaha Nebraska, U.S. 15 I3
Oman *country* 52 B5, 57 I5
Oman, Gulf of *gulf* 57 J4
Omdurman Sudan 49 H3
Omsk Russian Federation 54 E4
Onega, Lake *lake* 54 D2
Ontario *province* Canada 13 G5
Ontario, Lake *lake* 13 H6, 16 D4
Oostend Belgium 35 A7
Oporto Portugal 38 C3
Oral Kazakhstan 58 A4
Oran Algeria 48 E1
Orange France 37 H5
Orange *river* 51 B9
Oranjestad Aruba 21 G6
Örebro Sweden 31 C8
Oregon *state* U.S. 14 D2
Orinoco *river* 25 F1
Orivesi *lake* 31 F7
Orizaba, Volcán Pico de *volcano* 18 E4
Orkney Islands *islands* 28 B2, 32 D3
Orlando Florida, U.S. 17 C9
Orléans France 37 F3
Ortles *mountain* 40 C2
Oruro Bolivia 25 F5
Osaka Japan 67 G5
Osh Kyrgyzstan 59 E7
Oslo Norway 28 C2, 31 B8
Osnabrück Germany 35 C6
Ossa, Mount *mountain* 71 H6
Östersund Sweden 31 C6
Otra *river* 31 A8
Ottawa Canada 10 D4, 13 H6
Ouagadougou Burkina Faso 46 B3, 48 E4
Ouessant, Île d' *island* 36 C2
Ouésso Congo 50 B4
Oulu Finland 30 E5
Oulujärvi *lake* 31 E6
Ounasjoki *river* 30 E4
Ourense Spain 38 D2
Ouse *river* 33 E7
Outer Hebrides *islands* 28 B2, 32 B5
Oviedo Spain 38 E1
Oxford United Kingdom 33 E8
Ozero Issyk-Kul' *lake* 59 E6

P

Pacific Ocean *ocean* 12 C5, 14 C5, 24 D5, 26 B5, 63 H4, 67 G6 & I4, 72 D5, 73 bottom A5
Padua Italy 40 D3
Päijänne *lake* 31 E7
Pakistan *country* 52 B4, 59 C10
Palau *country* 68 A2
Palawan *island* 63 F3
Palembang Indonesia 62 D5
Palermo Italy 41 D8
Palikir Federated States of Micronesia 68 C2
Palma de Mallorca Spain 39 J4
Palmyra Atoll *U.S. dependent territory* 68 E2
Pamirs *mountains* 59 E7
Pampas *physical region* 27 D6
Pamplona Spain 39 G1
Panama *country* 10 D6, 19 I6
Panama Canal *canal* 19 I6
Panama City Panama 10 D6, 19 I6
Panama, Golfo de *gulf* 19 I6
Pantelleria *island* 41 C8
Papua New Guinea *country* 68 B3
Paracel Islands *disputed region* 62 E2
Paraguay *country* 22 C4, 26 E3
Paraguay *river* 26 F3
Paramaribo Suriname 22 C1, 25 H1
Paraná *river* 25 H5, 26 E4
Paranaíba *river* 25 H5
Paris France 28 B4, 37 F2
Parma Italy 40 C3
Parnaíba *river* 25 I3
Parry Islands *islands* 13 F2
Passau Germany 35 F9
Patagonia *physical region* 27 C9
Patos, Lagoa dos *lagoon* 25 H6
Pátra Greece 45 C9
Patuca *river* 19 H5
Pau France 36 E6
Pavlodar Kazakhstan 58 E4
Peace *river* 12 E4
Peak District *mountains* 33 E7
Pechora *river* 54 E2
Pecos *river* 15 G5
Pecs Hungary 42 D6
Peipus, Lake *lake* 43 G1
Pelagic Islands *islands* 41 D9
Pennine Alps *mountains* 40 B2
Pennines *mountains* 33 D6
Pennsylvania *state* U.S. 16 D5
Penzance United Kingdom 33 C10
Perm Russian Federation 54 D3
Perpignan France 37 G6
Perth Australia 70 D5
Perth United Kingdom 32 D5
Peru *country* 22 A3, 24 E4
Perugia Italy 40 D4
Pescara Italy 40 E5
Peshawar Pakistan 59 D8
Pevek Russian Federation 73 top C1
Philadelphia Pennsylvania, U.S. 16 E5
Philippines *country* 52 D5, 63 F3
Phnom Penh Cambodia 52 D5, 62 D3
Phoenix Arizona, U.S. 14 E5
Phoenix Islands *islands* 68 E2
Phuket Thailand 62 C4
Pico de Aneto *mountain* 39 H1
Pico Duarte *mountain* 21 F3
Piedmont *physical region* 17 C8
Pielinen *lake* 31 F6
Pierre South Dakota, U.S. 15 H2
Pietermaritzburg South Africa 51 D9
Pilcomayo *river* 26 E3
Píndus Mountains *mountains* 45 C8
Pineios *river* 45 C8
Ping *river* 62 C2
Piraeus Greece 45 D9
Pisa Italy 40 C4
Pit *river* 14 D2
Pitcairn Island *island* 69 G4
Pitcairn Islands *U.K. dependent territory* 69 G4
Pittsburgh Pennsylvania, U.S. 16 D5
Plata, Río de la *estuary* 26 F5
Platte *river* 15 H3
Plauer See *lake* 34 E5
Plenty, Bay of *bay* 72 E2
Ploiesti Romania 45 E5
Plovdiv Bulgaria 45 E7
Plymouth United Kingdom 33 D9
Po *river* 40 B3
Pobeda, Gora *mountain* 55 I2
Pobedy, Pik *mountain* 59 F6
see also Tomur Feng
Pointe-Noire Congo 50 A5
Poitiers France 36 E4
Poland *country* 28 C4, 42 D3
Pomeranian Bay *bay* 34 F5, 42 C3
Pontianak Indonesia 62 E5
Poopó, Lake *lake* 25 F5
Popocatépetl *volcano* 18 E4
Porpoise Bay *bay* 73 bottom E5
Port Augusta Australia 71 G5
Port-au-Prince Haiti 10 D6, 21 F4
Port-de-Paix Cuba 21 F3
Port Elizabeth South Africa 51 C10
Port-Gentil Gabon 50 A5
Portland Oregon, U.S. 14 D1
Port Louis Mauritius 51 F10
Port Moresby Papua New Guinea 68 B3
Porto Alegre Brazil 25 H6
Port-of-Spain Trinidad & Tobago 10 E6, 21 I6
Porto-Novo Benin 46 B3, 48 E5
Port Pirie Australia 71 G5
Port Said Egypt 49 H2
Portsmouth United Kingdom 33 E9
Port Sudan Sudan 49 I3
Portugal *country* 28 A5, 38 C3
Port-Vila Vanuatu 68 D3
Posadas Argentina 26 F4
Potsdam Germany 35 F6
Powell, Lake *lake* 15 F4
Poyang Hu China 65 I5
Poznan Poland 42 D4
Prague Czech Republic 28 C4, 42 C5
Praia Cape Verde 48 C3
Pretoria South Africa 46 D6, 51 C9
Prince Edward Island *province* Canada 13 J5
Prince George Canada 12 D4
Prince of Wales Island *island* (Australia) 71 H1
Prince of Wales Island *island* (Canada) 13 F2, 73 top A3
Prince Rupert Canada 12 C4
Princess Charlotte Bay *bay* 71 H1
Príncipe *island* 50 A4
Pripet *river* 43 G4
Pristina Serbia & Montenegro 45 C7
Prizren Serbia & Montenegro 45 C7
Prosna *river* 42 D4
Providence Rhode Island, U.S. 16 F5
Prut *river* 43 G6, 44 E4
Pskov, Lake *lake* 43 G1
Puebla Mexico 18 E4
Pueblo Colorado, U.S. 15 G4
Puerto Baquizero Moreno Galapagos Islands 24 E6
Puerto Rico *U.S. dependent territory* 10 E6, 21 H3
Pune India 61 B8
Punta Arenas Chile 27 C9
Purus *river* 25 F3
Pusan South Korea 66 D5
Putumayo *river* 24 E2
Pyongyang North Korea 52 E4, 66 C3
Pyramid Lake *lake* 14 D3
Pyrenees *mountains* 36 E6, 39 G1

Q

Qaanaaq Greenland 73 top B3
Qaidam Basin *physical region* 64 E3
Qaqortoq Greenland 73 top A5
Qaraghandy Kazakhstan 58 D5
Qatar *country* 54 B4, 57 H4
Qilian Shan *mountains* 65 F3
Qingdao China 65 I3
Qinghai Hu *lake* 65 F4
Qiqihar China 65 I1
Qom Iran 57 H2
Québec Canada 13 I6
Québec *province* Canada 13 H5
Queen Elizabeth Islands *islands* 13 F1, 73 top B3
Queensland *state* Australia 71 H3
Queenstown New Zealand 72 B5
Quetta Pakistan 59 D9
Quimperlé France 36 C2
Quito Ecuador 22 A2, 24 D2
Qyzylorda Kazakhstan 59 C6

R

Raab *river* 40 E2
Rába *river* 42 D6
Rabat Morocco 46 B1, 48 E1
Rainier, Mount *mountain* 14 D1
Rajang *river* 63 F5
Raleigh North Carolina, U.S. 17 D7
Ras Dashen *mountain* 49 I4
Ravenna Italy 40 D3
Ravi *river* 59 E9
Rawalpindi Pakistan 59 E8
Reading United Kingdom 33 E9
Recife Brazil 25 J3
Red Hill *mountain* 14 B6
Red *river* (Canada/U.S.) 15 H1
Red river *see* Song Da
Red *river* (U.S.) 15 H5
Red Sea *sea* 49 I2, 56 E4
Ree, Lough *lake* 33 B7
Reggio di Calabria Italy 41 E8
Regina Canada 12 E5
Reims France 37 G2
Rein *river* 40 B1
Reindeer Lake *lake* 13 F4
Rennes France 36 E2
Reno Nevada, U.S. 14 D3
Reno *river* 40 D3
Republican *river* 15 G3
Resistencia Argentina 26 E4
Réunion *French dependent territory* 46 E6, 51 E10
Reykjavik Iceland 28 A1, 30 E2
Rhaetian Alps *mountains* 40 C2
Rhine *river* 35 C9, 37 I2, 40 B1
Rhode Island *state* U.S. 16 F5
Rhodes *island* 28 D6, 45 F10
Rhodope Mountains *mountains* 45 D7
Rhön *mountains* 35 D8
Rhône *river* 37 H5, 40 B2
Richmond Virginia, U.S. 17 D6
Riga Latvia 28 D3, 43 F2
Riga, Gulf of *gulf* 43 F1
Rimini Italy 40 D4
Rio de Janeiro Brazil 25 I5
Riyadh Saudi Arabia 52 A4, 57 G4
Rockhampton Australia 71 I3
Rocky Mountains *mountains* 12 D3, 14 E1
Rogers, Mount *mountain* 17 C7
Romania *country* 28 D4, 44 D5
Rome Italy 28 C5, 40 D5
Roosevelt Island *island* 73 bottom C4
Rosario Argentina 26 E5
Roseau Dominica 21 I5
Ross Sea *sea* 73 bottom C4
Rostock Germany 34 E5
Rostov Russian Federation 54 C4
Røssvatnet *lake* 30 C5
Rotorua New Zealand 72 E2
Rotorua, Lake *lake* 72 E2
Rotterdam the Netherlands 35 A6
Rouen France 37 F2
Rovuma *river* 51 E7
Roxburgh New Zealand 72 B6
Ruapehu, Mount *mountain* 72 D3
Rufiji *river* 51 E6
Rügen *island* 34 F5
Ruse Bulgaria 45 E6
Russian Federation *country* 28 D3 & E2, 42 E3, 52 B2, 54–55
Ruvuma *river* 51 E6
Rwanda *country* 46 D4, 50 D5
Ryukyu Islands *islands* 52 E4, 66 E6

S

Saale *river* 35 E7
Saarbrücken Germany 35 B9
Saaremaa *island* 42 E1
Sabine *river* 15 I5
Sacramento *river* 14 D3
Sacramento California, U.S. 14 D3
Sacramento Mountains *mountains* 15 G5
Sado *island* 67 H3
Sagami-nada *inlet* 67 H5
Sahara *desert* 48 D3
Sahel *physical region* 48 D3
Saimaa *lake* 31 F7
Saint-Barthélémy *French dependent territory* 21 I4
St.-Denis Réunion 51 E10
St.-Étienne France 37 G4
St. George's Grenada 21 I6
St. Helena *island* 46 B5
St. Helens, Mount *mountain* 14 D1
St. John Canada 13 I6
St. John's Antigua & Barbuda 21 I4
St. John's Canada 13 J5
St. Kitts *island* 21 I4
St. Kitts & Nevis *country* 10 E6, 21 I4
St. Lawrence *river* 13 I5
St. Lawrence, Gulf of *gulf* 13 J5
St. Lawrence Island *island* 14 A4
St. Louis Missouri, U.S. 15 J3
St. Lucia *country* 10 E6, 21 I5
St. Malo, Golfo de *gulf* 36 D2
St. Martin *Dutch and French dependent territory* 21 I4
St.-Nazaire France 36 D3
St. Paul Minnesota, U.S. 15 I2
St. Petersburg Russian Federation 54 C2
St.-Philippe Réunion 51 E10
St. Pierre & Miquelon *island* 13 J5
St. Pierre & Miquelon *French dependent territory* 19 E4
St. Vincent *island* 21 J5
St. Vincent & the Grenadines *country* 10 E6, 21 I5
St. Vincent, Gulf *gulf* 71 G5
Sajama, Nevado *mountain* 25 F5
Sakai Japan 67 G5
Sakakawea, Lake *lake* 15 G1
Sakhalin *island* 52 E3, 55 J4
Salado *river* 26 D4, 27 D6
Salalah Oman 57 I6
Salamanca Spain 38 E3
Salem Oregon, U.S. 14 D1
Salerno Italy 41 E6
Salmon *river* 14 E2
Salmon River Mountains *mountains* 14 E2
Salt *river* 15 F5
Salt Lake City Utah, U.S. 14 E3
Salton Sea *lake* 14 D5
Salvador Brazil 25 J4
Salween *river* 62 C1
Salzach *river* 40 D1
Salzburg Austria 40 D1
Samar *island* 63 H3
Samara Russian Federation 54 D4
Samarqand Uzbekistan 59 D7
Samarra' Iraq 57 G2
Sambre *river* 35 A8
Samoa *country* 68 E3
Sámos *island* 45 E9
San *river* 42 E4
Sana Yemen 52 A5, 57 G6
San Antonio Texas, U.S. 15 H6
San Cristobal *island* 68 C3
San Cristóbal, Isla *island* 24 E6
Sancy, Puy de *mountain* 37 G4
San Diego California, U.S. 14 D5
San Francisco California, U.S. 14 C3
San Jose California, U.S. 14 C3
San José Costa Rica 10 C6, 19 H6
San Juan *river* 19 H5
San Juan Puerto Rico 21 H4
Sankt Gallen Switzerland 40 C1
San Marino *country* 28 C4, 40 C4
San Marino San Marino 40 D4
San Miguel de Tucumán Argentina 26 D4
San Rafael Argentina 26 C5
San Salvador El Salvador 10 C6, 19 G5
San Salvador, Isla *island* 24 D5
San Sebastián Spain 39 G1
Santa Cruz Canary Islands 48 D2
Santa Cruz *river* 27 C9
Santa Cruz Spain 48 D2
Santa Cruz, Isla *island* 24 E6
Santa Cruz Islands *islands* 68 C3
Santa Fé Argentina 26 E5
Santa Fe New Mexico, U.S. 15 G4
Santa Isabel *island* 68 C3
Santander Spain 39 F1
Santarém Portugal 38 C4
Santiago Chile 22 B5, 26 C5
Santiago Dominican Republic 21 F3
Santiago *island* 48 C3
Santiago de Compostela Spain 38 C1
Santiago de Cuba Cuba 20 E3
Santiago del Estero Argentina 26 D4
Santo Domingo Dominican Republic 10 E6, 21 G4
Santo Tomás *volcano* 24 D6
São Francisco *river* 25 I4
São Manuel *river* 25 G3
Saône *river* 37 H4
São Paulo Brazil 25 I5
Saõ Tiago Cape Verde 48 C3
São Tomé *island* 50 A4
São Tomé São Tomé & Príncipe 46 B4, 50 A5
São Tomé & Príncipe *country* 46 B4, 50 A4
Sapporo Japan 67 I2
Sarajevo Bosnia & Herzegovina 28 C5, 45 B6
Sardinia *island* 28 B5, 41 B6
Sartène Corsica 37 J6
Saskatchewan *province* Canada 12 E4
Saskatoon Canada 12 E5
Sassari Italy 41 B6
Saudi Arabia *country* 52 A4, 57 F5
Sault Ste. Marie Canada 13 G6
Sava *river* 40 E2, 44 B5
Savai'i *island* 68 E3
Savannah Georgia, U.S. 17 C8
Savannah *river* 17 C8
Saynshand Mongolia 65 G2
Schwäbische Alb *mountains* 35 C10
Schweriner See *lake* 34 E5
Scilly, Isles of *islands* 33 B10
Scotland *national region* United Kingdom 32 D5
Scutari, Lake *lake* 45 B7
Seattle Washington, U.S. 14 D1
Segre *river* 39 I2
Segura *river* 39 G5

Seine *river* 37 F2
Selenge Moron *river* 65 F1
Semarang Indonesia 62 E6
Sendai Japan 67 H3
Sendai wan *bay* 67 I4
Senegal *country* 48 A2, 48 C4
Senegal *river* 48 D3
Seoul South Korea 52 E4, 66 D4
Seram *island* 63 H5
Serbia & Montenegro *country* 28 D5, 45 C6
Serengeti Plain *physical region* 50 D5
Serra Geral *mountains* 25 H6
Setúbal Portugal 38 C4
Sevastopol' Ukraine 43 I6
Severn *river* 33 E8
Severnaya Zemlya *islands* 52 D1, 55 F2, 73 top D3
Sevier Lake *lake* 14 E3
Seville Spain 38 E5
Seychelles *country* 46 E4, 50 F3
Sfax Tunisia 49 F1
Shanghai China 65 I4
Shannon *river* 33 B8
Shan Plateau *plateau* 62 C1
Shasta, Mount *mountain* 14 D2
Shabeelle *river* 49 J5
Sheffield United Kingdom 33 E7
Shenyang China 65 I2
Shetland Islands *islands* 28 B2, 32 D2
Sheyenne *river* 15 H1
Shikoku *island* 67 F5
Shiraz Iran 57 H3
Siberia *physical region* 55 G3
Sicily *island* 28 C5, 41 D8
Sidra, Gulf of *gulf* 49 G2
Siem Reab Cambodia 62 D3
Siena Italy 40 C4
Sierra Leone *country* 46 A3, 48 C4
Sierra Madre *mountains* 19 F5
Sierra Madre del Sur *mountains* 18 E4
Sierra Madre Occidental *mountains* 18 C2
Sierra Madre Oriental *mountains* 18 D2
Sierra Nevada *mountains* 14 D3
Simpson Desert *desert* 71 G3
Singapore *country* 52 D5, 62 D5
Singapore Singapore 52 D5, 62 D5
Sioux Falls South Dakota, U.S. 15 H2
Siracusa Italy 41 E8
Siret *river* 44 E5
Siwalik Range *mountains* 60 C4
Sjaelland *island* 31 B10
Skellefte *river* 30 D5
Skopje Macedonia 28 D5, 45 C7
Skye *island* 32 C4
Slave *river* 12 E4
Slovakia *country* 28 C4, 42 D5
Slovenia *country* 28 C4, 40 E2
Smoky Hill *river* 15 H4
Smólikas *mountain* 45 C8
Snake *river* 14 D1 & E2
Snezka *mountain* 42 C4
Snowdon *mountain* 33 D8
Society Islands *islands* 69 F3
Socotra *island* 46 E3, 52 B5
Sofia Bulgaria 28 D5, 45 D7
Solomon Islands *country* 68 C3
Solway Firth *inlet* 33 D6
Somalia *country* 46 E4, 49 J5
Somerset Island *island* 13 F2
Somme *river* 37 F2
Song Da *river* 62 D1, 65 F6
Song Hong *river* 62 D1
Songhua Jiang *river* 65 I2
Songnim North Korea 66 C3
Sousse Tunisia 49 F1
South Africa *country* 46 C6, 51 B10
South America *continent* 22–27
Southampton United Kingdom 33 E9
South Australia *state* Australia 71 F4
South Carolina *state* U.S. 17 D7
South China Sea *sea* 63 F3, 65 I6
South Dakota *state* U.S. 15 G2
Southern Alps *mountains* 72 B5
Southern Cook Islands *islands* 68 E3
Southern Uplands *mountains* 33 D6
South Island *island* 72 B4
South Korea *country* 52 E4, 66 E4
South Magnetic Pole *pole* 73 bottom E5
South Platte *river* 15 G3
South Pole *pole* 73 bottom C3
South Saskatchewan *river* 12 E5
South Uist *island* 32 B4
Spain *country* 28 A5, 38 E4
Sparta Greece 45 D9
Spencer Gulf *gulf* 71 G5
Spey *river* 32 D4
Spiez Switzerland 40 B2
Split Croatia 45 B6

Spokane Washington, U.S. 14 E1
Spratly Islands *disputed region* 63 F3
Spree *river* 35 F7
Springfield Illinois, U.S. 17 A6
Sri Jayewardenepura Sri Lanka 52 C5, 61 C9
Sri Lanka *country* 52 C5, 61 C9
Srinagar India 60 B3
Stanley Falkland Islands 27 E9
Stavanger Norway 31 A8
Stewart Island *island* 72 B6
Stockholm Sweden 28 D3, 31 D8
Stoke-on-Trent United Kingdom 33 D8
Stony Tunguska *river* 55 F4
Storsjön Sweden 31 D8
Strasbourg France 37 I2
Stromboli *island* 41 E7
Sturt Stony Desert *desert* 71 H4
Stuttgart Germany 35 D9
Sucre Bolivia 22 C3, 25 F5
Sudan *country* 46 D3, 49 H3
Sudbury Canada 13 H6
Suez Egypt 49 H2
Suez Canal *canal* 49 H2
Sulu Sea *sea* 63 G4
Sumatra *island* 52 D6, 62 D5
Sunderland United Kingdom 33 E6
Sundsvall Sweden 31 D7
Superior, Lake *lake* 13 G6, 15 I1, 16 A3
Surabaya Indonesia 63 F6
Surat India 61 B6
Suriname *country* 22 C1, 25 G2
Sutlej *river* 59 E9
Suva Fiji 68 D3
Svalbard *Norwegian dependent territory* 73 top C4
Svartisen *glacier* 30 C5
Swansea United Kingdom 33 D9
Swaziland *country* 46 D6, 51 D9
Sweden *country* 28 C2, 31 C7
Switzerland *country* 28 C4, 40 B2
Sydney Australia 71 I5
Syr Darya *river* 59 C6
Syria *country* 52 A4, 57 F2
Syrian Desert *desert* 57 F2
Szczecin Poland 42 C3

T
Tabriz Iran 57 G1
Taegu South Korea 66 D4
Tagus *river* 38 C4, 38 E4
Tahat *mountain* 49 F2
Tahiti *island* 69 F3
Tahoe, Lake *lake* 14 D3
Taisetsu *mountain* 67 I1
Taiwan *country* 52 D4, 65 J6
Taiyuan China 65 H3
Ta'izz Yemen 57 G6
Tajikistan *country* 52 B4, 59 D7
Tajumulco, Volcán *volcano* 19 F5
Taklimakan Desert *desert* 59 F7
Tallahassee Florida, U.S. 17 C9
Tallinn Estonia 28 D3, 43 F1
Tampa Florida, U.S. 17 C9
Tampere Finland 31 E7
Tana, Lake *lake* 49 I4
Tanami Desert *desert* 71 F2
Tanga Tanzania 51 E6
Tanganyika, Lake *lake* 51 D6
Tangier Morocco 48 E1
Tangshan China 65 I3
Tanzania *country* 46 D4, 51 D6
Tapajós *river* 25 G3
Taranaki, Mount *mountain* 72 D3
Taranto Italy 41 F6
Taranto, Golfo di *gulf* 41 F6
Tarim He *river* 64 D3
Tarn *river* 37 G5
Tarragona Spain 39 I2
Tartu Estonia 43 F2
Tashkent Uzbekistan 52 B4, 59 D7
Tasman Bay *bay* 72 D3
Tasmania *island* 68 B5
Tasmania *state* Australia 71 H6
Tasman Sea *sea* 71 J6, 72 C4
Taupo, Lake *lake* 72 E2
Taurus Mountains *mountains* 56 E2
Tavira Portugal 38 D5
Te Anau, Lake *lake* 72 B5
Tees *river* 33 E6
Tegucigalpa Honduras 10 C6, 19 G5
Tehran Iran 52 B4, 57 H2
Tehuantepec, Golfo de *gulf* 19 F5
Tekapo, Lake *lake* 72 C5
Tenerife *island* 48 C2
Tengiz, Lake *lake* 58 D5
Tennessee *river* 17 C7
Tennessee *state* U.S. 17 A7
Teno *river* 30 E3
Tenojoki *river* 30 E3
Terni Italy 40 D5

Texas *state* U.S. 15 H6
Thailand *country* 52 D5, 62 D2
Thailand, Gulf of *gulf* 62 D3
Thames *river* 33 F3
Thar Desert *desert* 59 D10, 60 A5
Thessaloniki Greece 45 D8
Thimphu Bhutan 52 C4, 60 E5
Thionville France 37 H2
Thira *island* 45 E10
Thomson *seasonal river* 71 H3
Thunder Bay Canada 13 G6
Tianjin China 62 I3
Tiber *river* 40 D5
Tibet, Plateau of *plateau* 64 D4
Tien Shan *mountains* 59 E7, 64 C2
Tierra del Fuego *island* 27 D10
Tigris *river* 57 G3
Tijuana Mexico 18 B1
Tiksi Russian Federation 73 top D2
Tilburg the Netherlands 35 B7
Timisoara Romania 44 D5
Timor *island* 63 H6
Timor Sea *sea* 70 E1
Tirana Albania 28 D5, 45 C7
Tirso *river* 41 B6
Tisa *river* 44 C5
see also Tisza
Tisza *river* 42 E6
see also Tisa
Titicaca, Lake *lake* 25 F4
Tobago *island* 21 J6
Toba, Lake *lake* 62 C5
Tobol *river* 58 D5
Tocantins *river* 25 H4
Togo *country* 46 B3, 48 E4
Tokelau *N.Z. dependent territory* 68 E3
Tokyo Japan 52 E4, 67 H5
Toledo Spain 39 F4
Toledo Ohio, U.S. 16 C5
Tombigbee *river* 17 B8
Tombouctou Mali 48 E3
Tomsk Russian Federation 55 F4
Tomur Feng *mountain* 64 D2
see also Pobedy, Pik
Tonga *country* 68 D3
Tongatapu *island* 68 D3
Tonkin, Gulf of *gulf* 62 E2, 65 H6
Topeka Kansas, U.S. 15 I3
Torneträsk *lake* 30 D3
Tornionjoki *river* 30 E4
Toronto Canada 13 H6
Torrens, Lake *seasonal lake* 71 G4
Torreón Mexico 18 D2
Toulon France 37 H6
Toulouse France 37 F6
Tours France 37 F3
Townsville Australia 71 I2
Toyama Japan 67 G4
Transantarctic Mountains *mountains* 73 bottom B3
Transylvanian Alps *mountains* 44 D5
Trasimeno, Lago *lake* 40 D4
Trent *river* 33 E8
Trento Italy 40 C2
Trenton New Jersey, U.S. 16 E5
Trier Germany 35 B8
Trieste Italy 40 E3
Trinidad *island* 21 J6
Trinidad & Tobago *country* 10 E6, 21 J6
Tripoli Greece 45 D9
Tripoli Libya 46 C1, 49 F1
Tromsø Norway 30 D3, 73 top D5
Trondheim Norway 31 B6
Troyes France 37 G2
Trujillo Peru 24 D3
Tshuapa *river* 50 C5
Tsushima *islands* 66 E5
Tuamotu, Îles *islands* 69 F3
Tucson Arizona, U.S. 14 E6
Tuktoyaktuk Canada 73 top A1
Tulsa Oklahoma, U.S. 15 I4
Tunis Tunisia 46 C1, 49 F1
Tunisia *country* 46 C1, 49 F1
Turin Italy 40 B3
Turkana, Lake *lake* 50 E4
Turkey *country* 28 D5, 52 A4, 56 E1
Turkmenistan *country* 52 A4, 59 B7
Turks & Caicos Islands *U.K. dependent territory* 10 D5, 21 F3
Turku Finland 31 E8
Turpan Pendi *physical region* 64 E2
Tuvalu *country* 68 D2
Tuz, Lake *lake* 56 E1
Tweed *river* 33 D6
Tyne *river* 33 E6
Tyrrhenian Sea *sea* 41 C6

U
Ubangi *river* 49 G5, 50 B4
Ucayali *river* 24 E3
Uchiura wan *bay* 67 H2
Uele *river* 50 C4
Uganda *country* 46 D4, 50 D4
Ujung Pandang Indonesia 63 G6

Ukraine *country* 28 D4, 43 G5
Ulan Bator Mongolia 52 D3, 65 G2
Ulan-Ude Russian Federation 55 G5
Ullung Island *island* 66 E4
Ulm Germany 35 D9
Uluru *rocky outcrop* 71 F3
Umeå Sweden 31 D6
Ume *river* 31 D6
Ungava Bay *bay* 13 H4
United Arab Emirates *country* 52 B5, 57 H6
United Kingdom *country* 28 B3, 33 C6
United States of America *country* 10 B4, 14–17
Upper Lough Erne *lake* 33 B7
Uppsala Sweden 31 D8
Ural *river* 54 D4, 58 A5
Ural Mountains *mountains* 54 E3
Urgench Uzbekistan 59 C7
Urmia, Lake *lake* 57 G1
Uruguay *country* 22 C5, 26 F5
Uruguay *river* 22 C5, 26 F4
Urumqi China 64 E2
Ussuri *river* 65 J1
Ustyurt Plateau *plateau* 59 B6
Usumacinta *river* 19 G4
Utah *state* U.S. 14 E3
Utrecht the Netherlands 35 B6
Uys, Lake *lake* 64 E1
Uzbekistan *country* 52 B3, 59 C7

V
Vaal *river* 51 C9
Vaasa Finland 31 D6
Vaduz Liechtenstein 28 C4, 40 C2
Váh *river* 42 D5
Valdés, Península *peninsula* 27 D7
Valence France 37 H5
Valencia Spain 39 H4
Valencia Venezuela 25 F1
Valladolid Spain 38 E2
Valletta Malta 28 C6, 41 E9
Valparaíso Chile 26 C5
Vancouver Canada 12 C5
Vancouver Island *island* 12 C5
Vancouver, Mount *mountain* 12 C3
Van Diemen Gulf *gulf* 71 F1
Van, Lake *lake* 57 F1
Vänern *lake* 31 B8
Vantaa Finland 31 E8
Vanua Levu *island* 68 D3
Vanuatu *country* 68 C3
Varanasi India 60 D5
Varano, Lago di *lagoon* 40 F5
Vardar *river* 45 C7
Varna Bulgaria 45 F6
Västerås Sweden 31 C8
Vatican City *country* 28 C5, 40 D5
Vatnajökull *glacier* 30 F2
Vefsna *mountains* 30 C5
Venezuela *country* 22 B1, 25 F1
Venice Italy 40 D3
Venice, Gulf of *gulf* 40 D3
Verkoyansk Range *mountains* 55 H3
Vermont *state* U.S. 16 E4
Verona Italy 40 C3
Versailles France 37 F2
Vesterålen *islands* 28 D1, 30 C4
Vesuvius, Mount *volcano* 41 E6
Vicebsk Belarus 43 G2
Vicenza Italy 40 D3
Victoria Canada 12 C5
Victoria Seychelles 50 F3
Victoria *river* 71 F1
Victoria *state* Australia 71 H6
Victoria Falls *waterfall* 51 C8
Victoria Island *island* 12 E2, 73 top A2
Victoria, Lake *lake* 50 D5
Vienna Austria 28 C4, 40 F1
Vienne *river* 37 F4
Vientiane Laos 52 D5, 62 D2
Vietnam *country* 52 D5, 62 E3
Vignemale *mountain* 36 E6
Vigo Spain 38 C2
Vilnius Lithuania 28 D3, 43 F3
Viluyu *river* 55 H3
Vinson Massif *mountain* 73 bottom B3
Virginia *state* U.S. 17 D6
Virgin Islands *U.S. dependent territory* 21 I4
Visakhapatnam India 61 D7
Vistula *river* 42 D3
Vitu Levu *island* 68 D3
Vitim *river* 55 H4
Vitoria-Gasteiz Spain 39 G1
Vjoses *river* 45 C8
Vladivostok Russian Federation 55 I5
Vltava *river* 42 C5
Volga *river* 54 C4
Volgograd Russian Federation 54 C4
Volta, Lake *lake* 48 E4

Vorkuta Russian Federation 73 top E4
Vosges *mountains* 37 H3

W
Waal *river* 35 B6
Wabash *river* 17 B6
Waddenzee *sea* 34 B5
Waddington, Mount *mountain* 12 C5
Waiau *river* 72 B6
Waigeo, Pulau *island* 63 I5
Waikato *river* 72 D2
Wakatipu, Lake *lake* 72 B5
Wake Island *U.S. dependent territory* 68 C1
Walbrzych Poland 42 D4
Wales *national region* United Kingdom 33 D8
Wallis & Futuna *French dependent territory* 68 D3
Wanaka, Lake *lake* 72 B5
Wandel Sea *sea* 73 top C4
Wanganui *river* 72 D3
Warrego *seasonal river* 71 H4
Warsaw Poland 28 D3, 42 E4
Warta *river* 42 D3
Washington *state* U.S. 14 D1
Washington, D.C. District of Columbia, U.S. 10 D4, 17 D6
Washington, Mount *mountain* 16 E4
Waterford Republic of Ireland 33 C8
Watzmann *mountain* 35 F10
Weddell Sea *sea* 73 bottom B2
Wei *river* 65 G4
Wellington New Zealand 68 D5, 72 D4
Werra *river* 35 D8
Weser *river* 35 D6
Western Australia *state* Australia 70 D3
Western Dvina *river* 43 F2
Western Ghats *mountains* 61 B7
Western Sahara *disputed region* 46 A1, 48 D2
West Falkland *island* 27 E9
West Frisian Islands *islands* 34 B5
West Indies *islands* 20 E2
West Siberian Plain *physical region* 54 E3
West Virginia *state* U.S. 17 C6
Wexford Republic of Ireland 33 C8
Wheeler Peak *mountain* 15 G4
Whitehorse Canada 12 C3, 73 top A1
White Nile *river* 49 H4
White Sea *sea* 55 D2, 73 top E5
Whitney, Mount *mountain* 14 D4
Wichita Kansas, U.S. 15 H4
Wick United Kingdom 32 D4
Wicklow Mountains *mountains* 33 C8
Wiesbaden Germany 35 C8
Wight, Isle of *island* 33 E9
Wildspitze *mountain* 40 C2
Willemstad Netherlands Antilles 21 G6
Wilson, Mount *mountain* 15 F4
Windhoek Namibia 46 C6, 51 B8
Windward Islands *islands* 21 I6
Winnipeg Canada 13 F6
Winnipeg, Lake *lake* 13 F5
Winnipegosis, Lake *lake* 13 F5
Winterthur Switzerland 40 B1
Wisconsin *state* U.S. 16 A4
Wolf, Volcán *volcano* 24 D5
Wollaston Lake *lake* 13 F4

Wollongong Australia 71 I5
Woods, Lake *seasonal lake* 71 F2
Woods, Lake of the *lake* 13 F6, 15 I1
Worcester United Kingdom 33 E8
Wrangel Island *island* 53 G2, 55 I1, 73 top C1
Wrocław Poland 42 D4
Wuhan China 65 H5
Wuppertal Germany 35 C7
Würzburg Germany 35 D8
Wusuli Jiang *see* Ussuri
Wyndham Australia 70 E1
Wyoming *state* U.S. 15 F2

XYZ
Xi'an China 65 H4
Xiang Jiang *river* 65 H5
Xi Jiang *river* 65 H6
Xingu *river* 25 H3
Xining China 65 F4
Xixabangma Feng *mountain* 64 D5

Yablonovyy Range *mountains* 55 G5
Yaku-shima *island* 66 E6
Yakutsk Russian Federation 55 H3, 73 top E1
Yalong Jiang *river* 65 F4
Yalu *river* 65 J3
Yamaguchi Japan 66 E5
Yamoussoukro Ivory Coast 46 B3, 48 D4
Yamuna *river* 60 C4
Yangtze *see* Chang Jiang
Yaoundé Cameroon 46 C3, 49 F5
Yaqui *river* 18 C2
Yekaterinburg Russian Federation 54 D4
Yellowknife Canada 12 E3
Yellow river *see* Huang He
Yellow Sea *sea* 65 J3, 66 C4
Yellowstone *river* 15 G2
Yemen *country* 52 A5, 57 G6
Yenisey *river* 55 F3, 73 top E3
Yerevan Armenia 52 A4, 57 G1
Yokohama Japan 67 H5
Yonne *river* 37 G2
York United Kingdom 33 E7
Yucatan Channel *channel* 19 G3, 20 B2
Yukon *river* 12 C3
Yukon Territory *province* Canada 12 C3

Sakhalin Russian Federation 55 J4
Zagreb Croatia 28 C4, 44 A5
Zagros Mountains *mountains* 57 H3
Zahedan Iran 57 J3
Zákynthos *island* 45 C9
Zambezi *river* 51 C7
Zambia *country* 46 C5, 51 C7
Zamboanga Philippines 63 G4
Zanzibar Tanzania 51 E6
Zanzibar *island* 51 E6
Zaragoza Spain 39 H2
Zaria Nigeria 49 F4
Zaysan, Lake *lake* 58 F5
Zeebrugge Belgium 35 A7
Zhengzhou China 65 H4
Zimbabwe *country* 46 D5, 51 C8
Zi Shui *river* 65 H5
Zufar *physical region* 57 I5
Zugspitze *mountain* 35 D10, 40 C1
Zürich Switzerland 40 B1
Zürichsee *lake* 40 B2
Zwolle the Netherlands 35 B6

Acknowledgments

The Publisher would like to thank the following for permission to reproduce their material. Every care has been taken to trace copyright holders. However, if there have been unintentional omissions or failure to trace copyright holders, we apologize and will, if informed, endeavor to make corrections in any future edition.

Key: b = bottom, c = center, l = left, r = right, t = top

2tr George H. H. Huey/Corbis; 2br Getty Images; 3tl Robin Smith/Getty Images; 3tr Frans Lemmens/Getty Images; 3bl Torleif Svensson/Corbis; 3cr Australian Picture Library/Corbis; 4bl Alison Wright/Corbis; 4bcl Randy Wells/Corbis; 4bcr Galen Rowell/Corbis; 4br Bob Krist/Corbis; 4–5tc ImageState/Alamy; 5bl Getty Images; 11tl Nathan Benn/Corbis; 11cl Darwin Wiggett/Corbis; 11br Brooke Slezak/Corbis; 13 David Stoecklein/Corbis; 16 Joseph Sohm; Visions of America/Corbis; 19 Danny Lehman/Corbis; 21 Don Herbert/Getty Images; 23tl Will & Deni McIntyre/Getty Images; 23bl Jerry Alexander/Getty Images; 23tr Travel Pix/Getty Images; 24bl Getty Images; 27 Hubert Stadler/Corbis; 28–29bc John Lamb/Getty Images; 28br Connie Coleman/Getty Images; 31 Dallas and John Heaton/Corbis; 32 Getty Images; 34 Doug Armand/Getty Images; 37 Getty Images; 39 Buddy Mays/Corbis; 41 Peter Adams/Getty Images; 43 ML Sinibaldi/Corbis; 44 Michael Freeman/Corbis; 46–47tc Wolfgang Kaehler/Corbis; 47cl Tibor Bognár/Corbis; 47br Angelo Cavalli/Getty Images; 48 Nik Wheeler/Corbis; 50 Torleif Svensson/Corbis; 53bl Craig Lovell/Corbis; 53br Peter Adams/Getty Images; 55 Wolfgang Kaehler/Corbis; 56 Fergus O'Brien/Getty Images; 58 Robert Harding Picture Library Ltd/Alamy; 60 Frans Lemmens/Getty Images; 62 Jochem D. Wijnands/Getty Images; 67 Frank Leather; Eye Ubiquitous/Corbis; 68 Peter Adams/Getty Images; 69br Nicholas DeVore/Getty Images; 70 Australian Picture Library/Corbis; 74 V.C.L./Getty Images; Back cover br Travel Pix/Getty Images.